joe

5/76

Profusely illus.
color fronts.

S

PICASSO
Forty Years of his Art

The Race.   1922. Tempera on wood, 12⅞ x 16¼ inches. Catalog no. 167.

PICASSO

Forty Years of his Art

Edited by Alfred H. Barr, Jr.

with two statements by the artist

In collaboration with The Art Institute of Chicago

The Museum of Modern Art, New York

CONTENTS

FOREWORD

and Acknowledgments

This exhibition of the art of Pablo Picasso is a joint undertaking of the Art Institute of Chicago and the Museum of Modern Art in New York. As long ago as 1931 the Museum of Modern Art had begun work on a Picasso exhibition but for various reasons it had to be postponed. These disappointments however have proved in the end to be fortunate, for in the past eight years Picasso has produced works which greatly enrich a retrospective exhibition. Furthermore, the support and influential sponsorship provided by the Chicago institution have made possible a more complete exhibition than would have been undertaken by either museum alone.

Any retrospective of the work of so fecund and versatile a genius as Picasso can lay no claims to completeness even with over three hundred items in its catalog. Those who may use this book as a survey of his art must make allowances for certain omissions and certain redundancies which are unavoidable in an exhibition. Fortunately a large proportion of the European loans were brought to this country before the outbreak of the war; possibly fifteen other loans from England and France may yet be added in spite of the war, but a few important loans will probably have to be abandoned. Most of the doubtful European loans are listed and some are illustrated so that the original symmetry of the exhibition can at least be preserved in this catalog. The most serious disappointment caused by the war is the absence of a large and very important group of Picasso's recent sculpture some of which was being cast especially for the show. Even the photographs of these have been delayed. The exhibition is however the most comprehensive presentation of Picasso's work so far assembled and includes almost all of his eight or ten capital works.

This publication and in large part the exhibition which it records are the work of the staff of the Museum of Modern Art, though the Art Institute has rendered valuable service in giving information and supporting requests for loans. It is hoped that in the future the two museums may be partners in another important exhibition for which the Chicago staff will be primarily responsible.

ALFRED H. BARR, JR., Director, The Museum of Modern Art
DANIEL CATTON RICH, Director of Fine Arts, The Art Institute of Chicago

ACKNOWLEDGMENTS

The President and Trustees of the Museum of Modern Art and of the Art Institute of Chicago wish to thank those who have lent to the exhibition and, in addition, those who have generously rendered assistance: Mr. Gordon Washburn, director of the Albright Art Gallery; Mr. Laurance P. Roberts, director of the Brooklyn Museum; Mr. Edward Forbes, director, and Mr. Paul J. Sachs, associate director, of the Fogg Art Museum; Mr. William M. Milliken, director, and Mr. Henry Sayles Francis, curator of paintings, of the Cleveland Museum of Art; Mr. Philip R. Adams, director of the Columbus Gallery of Fine Arts; Mr. A. Everett Austin, Jr., director of the Wadsworth Atheneum; Mr. A. E. Gallatin, director of the Museum of Living Art, New York University; Baroness Hilla Rebay, curator of the Solomon R. Guggenheim Foundation; Mr. Jere Abbott, director of the Smith College Museum of Art; Mr. Fiske Kimball, director, and Mr. Henri Marceau, assistant director, of the Philadelphia Museum of Art; Mr. Alexander Dorner, director of the Museum of the Rhode Island School of Design; Mrs. Grace L. McCann Morley, director of the San Francisco Museum of Art; Mr. Blake-More Godwin, director of the Toledo Museum of Art; Mr. Duncan Phillips, director of the Phillips Memorial Gallery; Mr. Francis Henry Taylor, director of the Worcester Art Museum; Mr. Valentine Dudensing; Mr. Jean Goriany; Mr. Sidney Janis; Miss Janice Loeb; Mr. D. H. Kahnweiler; Miss Dora Maar; Miss Agnes Mongan; Miss Dorothy Odenheimer; Miss Agnes Roullier; Mr. Jaime Sabartes; Mrs. George Palen Snow; Mr. Carl O. Schniewind; Mr. James Johnson Sweeney; The Spanish Refugee Relief Campaign; Mr. Carl Zigrosser.

The exhibition is especially indebted to Mrs. Meric Callery for making accessible the list of Picassos in American collections which she has assembled for the second volume of Mr. Christian Zervos' *catalogue raisonné* of Picasso's work, and for her help in Paris; to Mr. Zervos for access to his unpublished files of photographs; and to Mr. Paul Rosenberg, who most generously put at the service of the exhibition his photographic files and his great store of information.

EXHIBITION STAFF

The following members of the staff of the Museum of Modern Art have worked directly upon the exhibition and catalog: Monroe Wheeler, director of publications; Dorothy C. Miller, assistant curator of painting and sculpture, and her assistant, Elise Van Hook; Dorothy H. Dudley, registrar, and her assistant, Dorothy C. Knowles; Sarah Newmeyer, publicity director; Beaumont Newhall, librarian; Harriet Dyer Adams, acting curator of prints; Paul Magriel, special librarian in charge of the American Dance Archives; Lenore Browning, secretary to the director; Margaret Scolari, assistant to the director in Paris.

LENDERS TO THE EXHIBITION

Mr. and Mrs. Walter C. Arensberg, Hollywood; Mr. Lee A. Ault, New York; Mr. A. Bellanger, Paris; Mr. and Mrs. Walter S. Brewster, Chicago; Mr. John Nicholas Brown, Providence; Mrs. Meric Callery, Boulogne-sur-Seine; Mr. Walter P. Chrysler, Jr., New York; Mr. and Mrs. Henry Clifford, Philadelphia; Mr. Frank Crowninshield, New York; Mr. Marcel Fleischmann, Zurich; Mrs. John W. Garrett, Baltimore; Mrs. Charles B. Goodspeed, Chicago; Mr. Philip L. Goodwin, New York; Mr. A. Conger Goodyear, New York; Mr. Jean Goriany, New York; Mr. and Mrs. William Averell Harriman, New York; Mrs. Patrick C. Hill, New Haven; Mr. Sidney Janis, New York; Mr. T. Catesby Jones, New York; Mr. Alphonse Kann, Saint-Germain-en-Laye; Miss Harriet Levy, San Francisco; The Lewisohn Collection, New York; Mrs. Charles J. Liebman, New York; Mr. Pierre Loeb, Paris; Mr. George Macy, New York; Mr. and Mrs. Chauncey McCormick, Chicago; Mr. Henry P. McIlhenny, Germantown, Pennsylvania; Mr. George L. K. Morris, New York; Mrs. Ray Slater Murphy, New York; Mr. J. B. Neumann, New

STATEMENT BY PICASSO : 1923

Photograph by Man Ray, about 1922

The following statement was made in Spanish to Marius de Zayas. Picasso approved de Zayas' manuscript before it was translated into English and published in The Arts, *New York, May, 1923, under the title* Picasso Speaks. *It is here reprinted with the kind permission of Forbes Watson, editor of* The Arts *(see bibl., item 1).*

I can hardly understand the importance given to the word *research* in connection with modern painting. In my opinion to search means nothing in painting. To find, is the thing. Nobody is interested in following a man who, with his eyes fixed on the ground, spends his life looking for the pocketbook that fortune should put in his path. The one who finds something no matter what it might be, even if his intention were not to search for it, at least arouses our curiosity, if not our admiration.

Among the several sins that I have been accused of committing, none is more false than the one that I have, as the principal objective in my work, the spirit of research. When I paint my object is to show what I have found and not what I am looking for. In art intentions are not sufficient and, as we say in Spanish: love must be proved by facts and not by reasons. What one does is what counts and not what one had the intention of doing.

We all know that art is not truth. Art is a lie that makes us realize truth, at least the truth that is given us to understand. The artist must know the manner whereby to convince others of the truthfulness of his lies. If he only shows in his work that he has searched, and re-searched, for the way to put over his lies, he would never accomplish anything.

The idea of research has often made painting go astray, and made the artist lose himself in mental lucubrations. Perhaps this has been the principal fault of modern art. The spirit of research has poisoned those who have not fully understood all the positive and conclusive elements in modern art and has made them attempt to paint the invisible and, therefore, the unpaintable.

They speak of naturalism in opposition to modern painting. I would like to know if anyone has ever seen a natural work of art. Nature and art, being two different things, cannot be the same thing. Through art we express our conception of what nature is not.

Velasquez left us his idea of the people of his epoch. Undoubtedly they were different from what he painted them, but we cannot conceive a Philip IV in any other way than the one Velasquez painted. Rubens also made a portrait of the same king and in Rubens' portrait he seems to be quite another person. We believe in the one painted by Velasquez, for he convinces us by his right of might.

From the painters of the origins, the primitives, whose work is obviously different from nature, down to those artists who, like David, Ingres and even Bouguereau, believed in painting nature as it is, art has always been art and not nature. And from the point of view of art there are no concrete or abstract forms, but only forms which are more or less convincing lies. That those lies are necessary to our mental selves is beyond any doubt, as it is through them that we form our esthetic point of view of life.

Cubism is no different from any other school of painting. The same principles and the same elements are common to all. The fact that for a long time cubism has not been understood and that even today there are people who cannot see anything in it, means nothing. I do not read English, an English book is a blank book to me. This does not mean that the English language does not exist, and why should I blame anybody else but myself if I cannot understand what I know nothing about?

I also often hear the word evolution. Repeatedly I am asked to explain how my painting evolved. To me there is no past or future in art. If a work of art cannot live always in the present it must not be considered at all. The art of the Greeks, of the Egyptians, of the great painters who lived in other times, is not an art of the past; perhaps it is more alive today than it ever was. Art does not evolve by itself, the ideas of people change and with them their mode of expression. When I hear people speak of the evolution of an artist, it seems to me that they are considering him standing between two mirrors that face each other and reproduce his image an infinite number of times, and that they contemplate the successive images of one mirror as his past, and the images of the other mirror as his future, while his real image is taken as his present. They do not consider that they all are the same images in different planes.

Variation does not mean evolution. If an artist varies his mode of expression this only means that he has changed his manner of thinking, and in changing, it might be for the better or it might be for the worse.

The several manners I have used in my art must not be considered as an evolution, or as steps toward an unknown ideal of painting. All I have ever made was made for the present and with the hope that it will always remain in the present. I have never taken into consideration the spirit of research. When I have found something to express, I have done it without thinking of the past or of the future. I do not believe I have used radically different elements in the different manners I have used in painting. If the subjects I have wanted to express have suggested different ways of expression I have never hesitated to adopt them. I have never made trials nor experiments. Whenever I had something to say, I have said it in the manner in which I have felt it ought to be said. Different motives inevitably require different methods of expression. This does not imply either evolution or progress, but an adaptation of the idea one wants to express and the means to express that idea.

Arts of transition do not exist. In the chronological history of art there are periods which are more positive, more complete than others. This means that there are periods in which there are better artists than in others. If the history of art could be graphically represented, as in a chart used by a nurse to mark the changes of temperature of her patient, the same silhouettes of mountains would be shown, proving that in art there is no ascendant progress, but that it follows certain ups and downs that might occur at any time. The same occurs with the work of an individual artist.

Many think that cubism is an art of transition, an experiment which is to bring ulterior results. Those who think that way have not understood it. Cubism is not either a seed or a foetus, but an art dealing primarily with forms, and when a form is realized it is there to live its own life. A mineral substance, having geometric formation, is not made so for transitory purposes, it is to remain what it is and will always have its own form. But if we are to apply the law of evolution and transformism to art, then we have to admit that all art is transitory. On the contrary, art does not enter into these philosophic absolutisms. If cubism is an art of transition I am sure that the only thing that will come out of it is another form of cubism.

Mathematics, trigonometry, chemistry, psychoanalysis, music, and whatnot, have been related to cubism to give it an easier interpretation. All this has been pure literature, not to say nonsense, which brought bad results, blinding people with theories.

Cubism has kept itself within the limits and limitations of painting, never pretending to go beyond it. Drawing, design and color are understood and practiced in cubism in the same spirit and manner that they are understood and practiced in all other schools. Our subjects might be different, as we have introduced into painting objects and forms that were formerly ignored. We have kept our eyes open to our surroundings, and also our brains.

We give to form and color all their individual significance, as far as we can see it; in our subjects we keep the joy of discovery, the pleasure of the unexpected; our subject itself must be a source of interest. But of what use is it to say what we do when everybody can see it if he wants to?

STATEMENT BY PICASSO : 1935

Christian Zervos put down these remarks of Picasso immediately after a conversation with him at Boisgeloup, his country place, in 1935. When Zervos wanted to show Picasso his notes Picasso replied: "You don't need to show them to me. The essential thing in our period of weak morale is to create enthusiasm. How many people have actually read Homer? All the same the whole world talks of him. In this way the homeric legend is created. A legend in this sense provokes a valuable stimulus. Enthusiasm is what we need most, we and the younger generation."

Zervos reports however that Picasso did actually go over the notes and approved them informally. They were published under the title Conversation avec Picasso *in "Cahiers d'Art," 1935, volume 10, number 10, pages 173-8. The following translation is based on one by Myfanwy Evans.*

We might adopt for the artist the joke about there being nothing more dangerous than implements of war in the hands of generals. In the same way, there is nothing more dangerous than justice in the hands of judges, and a paintbrush in the hands of a painter. Just think of the danger to society! But today we haven't the heart to expel the painters and poets from society because we refuse to admit to ourselves that there is any danger in keeping them in our midst.

It is my misfortune — and probably my delight — to use things as my passions tell me. What a miserable fate for a painter who adores blondes to have to stop himself putting them into a picture because they don't go with the basket of fruit! How awful for a painter who loathes apples to have to use them all the time because they go so well with the cloth. I put all the things I like into my pictures. The things — so much the worse for them; they just have to put up with it.

In the old days pictures went forward toward completion by stages. Every day brought something new. A picture used to be a sum of additions. In my case a picture is a sum of destructions. I do a picture — then I destroy it. In

Photograph by Man Ray, 1935

the end, though, nothing is lost: the red I took away from one place turns up somewhere else.

It would be very interesting to preserve photographically, not the stages, but the metamorphoses of a picture. Possibly one might then discover the path followed by the brain in materializing a dream. But there is one very odd thing — to notice that basically a picture doesn't change, that the first "vision" remains almost intact, in spite of appearances. I often ponder on a light and a dark when I have put them into a picture; I try hard to break them up by interpolating a color that will create a different effect. When the work is photographed, I note that what I put in to correct my first vision has disappeared, and that, after all, the photographic image corresponds with my first vision before the transformation I insisted on.

A picture is not thought out and settled beforehand. While it is being done it changes as one's thoughts change. And when it is finished, it still goes on changing, according to the state of mind of whoever is looking at it. A picture lives a life like a living creature, undergoing the changes imposed on us by our life from day to day. This is natural enough, as the picture lives only through the man who is looking at it.

At the actual time that I am painting a picture I may think of white and put down white. But I can't go on working all the time thinking of white and painting it. Colors, like features, follow the changes of the emotions. You've seen the sketch I did for a picture with all the colors indicated on it. What is left of them? Certainly the white I thought of and the green I thought of are there in the picture, but not in the places I intended, nor in the same quantities. Of course, you can paint pictures by matching up different parts of them so that they go quite nicely together, but they'll lack any kind of drama.

I want to get to the stage where nobody can tell how a picture of mine is done. What's the point of that? Simply that I want nothing but emotion to be given off by it.

Work is a necessity for man.

A horse does not go between the shafts of its own accord.

Man invented the alarm clock.

When I begin a picture, there is somebody who works with me. Toward the end, I get the impression that I have been working alone — without a collaborator.

When you begin a picture, you often make some pretty discoveries. You must be on guard against these. Destroy the thing, do it over several times. In each destroying of a beautiful discovery, the artist does not really suppress it, but rather transforms it, condenses it, makes it more substantial. What comes out in the end is the result of discarded finds. Otherwise, you become your own connoisseur. I sell myself nothing!

Actually, you work with few colors. But they seem like a lot more when each one is in the right place.

Abstract art is only painting. What about drama?

There is no abstract art. You must always start with something. Afterward you can remove all traces of reality. There's no danger then, anyway, because the idea of the object will have left an indelible mark. It is what started the artist off, excited his ideas, and stirred up his emotions. Ideas and emotions will in the end be prisoners in his work. Whatever they do, they can't escape from the picture. They form an integral part of it, even when their presence is no longer discernible. Whether he likes it or not, man is the instrument of nature. It forces on him its character and appearance. In my Dinard pictures and in my Pourville pictures I expressed very much the same vision. However, you yourself have noticed how different the atmosphere of those painted in Brittany is from those painted in Normandy, because you recognized the light of the Dieppe cliffs. I didn't *copy* this light nor did I pay it any special attention. I was simply soaked in it· My eyes saw it and my subconscious registered what they saw: my hand fixed the impression. One cannot go against nature. It is stronger than the strongest man. It is pretty much to our interest to be on good terms with it! We may allow ourselves certain liberties, but only in details.

Nor is there any "figurative" and "non-figurative" art. Everything appears to us in the guise of a "figure." Even in metaphysics ideas are expressed by means of symbolic "figures." See how ridiculous it is then to think of painting without "figuration." A person, an object, a circle are all "figures"; they react on us more or less intensely. Some are nearer our sensations and produce emotions that touch our affective faculties; others appeal more directly to the intellect. They all should be allowed a place because I find my spirit has quite as much need of emotion as my senses. Do you think it concerns me that a particular picture of mine represents two people? Though these two people once existed for me, they exist no longer. The "vision" of them gave me a preliminary emotion; then little by little their actual presences became blurred; they developed into a fiction and then disappeared altogether, or rather they were transformed into all kinds of problems. They are no longer two people, you see, but forms and colors: forms and colors that have taken on, meanwhile, the *idea* of two people and preserve the vibration of their life.

I deal with painting as I deal with things. I paint a window just as I look out of a window. If an open window looks wrong in a picture, I draw the curtain and shut it, just as I would in my own room. In painting, as in life, you must act directly. Certainly, painting has its conventions, and it is essential to reckon with them. Indeed, you can't do anything else. And so you always ought to keep an eye on real life.

The artist is a receptacle for emotions that come from all over the place: from the sky, from the earth, from a scrap of paper, from a passing shape, from a spider's web. That is why we must not discriminate between things. Where things are concerned there are no class distinctions. We must pick out what is good for us where we can find it — except from our own works. I have a horror of copying myself. But when I am shown a portfolio of old drawings, for instance, I have no qualms about taking anything I want from them.

When we invented cubism we had no intention whatever of inventing cubism. We wanted simply to express what was in us. Not one of us drew up a plan of campaign, and our friends, the poets, followed our efforts attentively, but they never dictated to us. Young painters today often draw up a program to follow, and apply themselves like diligent students to performing their tasks.

The painter goes through states of fullness and evacuation. That is the whole secret of art. I go for a walk in the forest of Fontainebleau. I get "green" indigestion. I must get rid of this sensation into a picture. Green rules it. A painter paints to unload himself of feelings and visions. People seize on painting to cover up their nakedness. They get what they can wherever they can. In the end I don't believe they get anything at all. They've simply cut a coat to the measure of their own ignorance. They make everything, from God to a picture, in their own image. That is why the picture-hook is the ruination of a painting — a painting which has always a certain significance, at least as much as the man who did it. As soon as it is bought and hung on a wall, it takes on quite a different kind of significance, and the painting is done for.

Academic training in beauty is a sham. We have been deceived, but so well deceived that we can scarcely get back even a shadow of the truth. The beauties of the Parthenon, Venuses, Nymphs, Narcissuses, are so many lies. Art is not the application of a canon of beauty but what the instinct and the brain can conceive beyond any canon. When we love a woman we don't start measuring her limbs. We love with our desires — although everything has been done to try and apply a canon even to love. The Parthenon is really only a farmyard over which someone put a roof; colonnades and sculptures were added because there were people in Athens who happened to be working, and wanted to express themselves. It's not what the artist *does* that counts, but what he *is*. Cézanne would never have interested me a bit if he had lived and thought like Jacques Emile Blanche, even if the apple he painted had been ten times as beautiful. What forces our interest is Cézanne's anxiety — that's Cézanne's lesson; the torments of van Gogh — that is the actual drama of the man. The rest is a sham.

Everyone wants to understand art. Why not try to understand the song of a bird? Why does one love the night, flowers, everything around one, without trying to understand them? But in the case of a painting people have to *understand*. If only they would realize above all that an artist works of necessity, that he himself is only a trifling bit of the world, and that no more importance should be attached to him than to plenty of other things which please us in the world, though we can't explain them. People who try to explain pictures are usually barking up the wrong tree. Gertrude Stein joyfully announced to me the other day that she had at last understood what my picture of the three musicians was meant to be. It was a still life!

How can you expect an onlooker to live a picture of mine as I lived it? A picture comes to me from miles away: who is to say from how far away I sensed it, saw it, painted it; and yet the next day I can't see what I've done myself. How can anyone enter into my dreams, my instincts, my desires, my thoughts, which have taken a long time to mature and to come out into the daylight, and above all grasp from them what I have been about — perhaps against my own will?

With the exception of a few painters who are opening new horizons to painting, young painters today don't know which way to go. Instead of taking up our researches in order to react clearly against us, they are absorbed with bringing the past back to life — when truly the whole world is open before us, everything waiting to be done, not just redone. Why cling desperately to everything that has already fulfilled its promise? There are miles of painting "in the manner of"; but it is rare to find a young man working in his own way.

Does he wish to believe that man can't repeat himself? To repeat is to run counter to spiritual laws; essentially escapism.

I'm no pessimist, I don't loathe art, because I couldn't live without devoting all my time to it. I love it as the only end of my life. Everything I do connected with it gives me intense pleasure. But still, I don't see why the whole world should be taken up with art, demand its credentials, and on that subject give free rein to its own stupidity. Museums are just a lot of lies, and the people who make art their business are mostly imposters. I can't understand why revolutionary countries should have more prejudices about art than out-of-date countries! We have infected the pictures in museums with all our stupidities, all our mistakes, all our poverty of spirit. We have turned them into petty and ridiculous things. We have been tied up to a fiction, instead of trying to sense what inner life there was in the men who painted them. There ought to be an absolute dictatorship . . . a dictatorship of painters . . . a dictatorship of one painter . . . to suppress all those who have betrayed us, to suppress the cheaters, to suppress the tricks, to suppress mannerisms, to suppress charm, to suppress history, to suppress a heap of other things. But common sense always gets away with it. Above all, let's have a revolution against that! The true dictator will always be conquered by the dictatorship of common sense . . . and maybe not!

Catalog
and Illustrations

1881:   Born Malaga, Spain.

1896:   Family moved to Barcelona; studied at Barcelona and Madrid Academies.

1896-1901: Early work, Barcelona, Madrid, Paris (1900-1901).

1901(late)-1904(early): "Blue" period, Paris, Barcelona. Has lived since 1904 in Paris except during the summers.

1905:   "Harlequin" period. Sculpture; prints.

1905(late)-1906: "Rose" period, Paris, Gosol.

1907-1908: "Negro" period.

1909-1912: "Analytical" cubism.

1912-1914: Pasted paper *(papier collé)*; relief constructions in wood.

1913, on: "Synthetic" cubism, a method of composition which he has used with modifications and together with other styles almost to the present time.

1915:   Realistic portrait drawings mark first departure from cubist technique.

1917:   To Italy for a month with Russian Ballet for which he made designs until 1924.

1918-1925: "Classic" style which he continues to use in prints and drawings almost to the present time. Married (1918); son born (1920); portraits.

1925 to the present time: Picasso has invented or adapted a great variety of styles and techniques in many media. Much of his work, especially since 1925, in its fantastic or grotesque character suggests sympathy with the Surrealists who have been among his friends in recent years.

1928, on: Sculpture and constructions.

1937:   *Guernica* mural.

(A chronology of Picasso's Paris and summer addresses is given on page 197.)

The catalog is arranged in approximately chronological order. Every effort has been made to represent the full range and variety of Picasso's art but there are certain unavoidable omissions, notably among his portraits and early works, which the artist did not want represented, and in the sculpture of the last twelve years which could not be included because of the European War.

KEY

Oil paintings are on canvas, so far as known, unless otherwise noted.

(dated) following a date means that the date appears on the picture.

In dimensions, height precedes width.

Abbreviations:

bibl.   refers to the numbered bibliography, page 200.

G.   refers to the *catalogue raisonné* of Picasso's prints by Bernhard Geiser (bibl. 91).

K.   following a date means that the date has been given or confirmed by D. H. Kahnweiler.

P.   following a date means that Picasso has confirmed the date.

Z.   refers to *Pablo Picasso* by Christian Zervos, Vol. I, cataloging works from 1895 to 1906 (bibl. 231).

2

1. Roses. 1898. Oil, 14¼ x 16¾ inches. Lent by the Bignou Gallery. Reproduced Z., pl. 6.

2. The Artist's Sister. Barcelona, 1899 (P). Oil, 59 x 39½ inches. Lent by the artist.

Pablo Ruiz Picasso was born on October 25, 1881, in Malaga on the Mediterranean coast of Spain. His father, José Ruiz Blasco, was an art teacher who, some fifteen years after Picasso's birth, became a professor at the Barcelona Academy of Fine Arts; his mother was Maria Picasso. As is customary in Spain Picasso used his mother's name and after 1901 dropped Ruiz entirely from his signature.

Picasso from a very early age showed extraordinary talent. His father encouraged and guided his studies until in 1896 he passed the entrance tests for the Barcelona Academy, taking only one day for an examination so difficult that a whole month was ordinarily allowed for its completion. A few months later he repeated this prodigious performance at Madrid. But he soon grew so bored with the sterile atmosphere of the Madrid Academy that he returned to Barcelona to set himself up as an independent artist at the age of sixteen.

At first Picasso painted studies of beggars as Spanish in their intense sombre realism as a Zurburan or early Velasquez. His Roses of 1898 (no. 1) is still timid technically, but the portrait of his sister (no. 2) of the following year shows a considerable mastery of soft sweeping forms not far removed, except for the silvery tone, from the late style of Renoir. All during this period of rapid development Picasso was drawing incessantly, filling sketch books with notes on the street scenes and night life of Barcelona, caricatures and portrait studies, among them the self-portrait in crayon made during a visit to Madrid (no. 3). It is significant that among these pre-Paris studies are certain works which anticipate the concern for human suffering and poverty which was to appear so often in his work during the first five years of the 20th century.

3

3. Self Portrait. Madrid, 1900(Z). Conté crayon, 13½ x 6 inches. Lent by J. Thannhauser.

5

Picasso came to Paris for the first time late in October 1900, within a few days of his 19th birthday. There he continued to paint cabaret and street scenes of which the sultry Moulin de la Galette (no. 5) is the most important. This picture and drawings of the same period (no. 4) suggest the influence of such painters as Steinlen and Toulouse-Lautrec. He returned to Spain before Christmas, but Paris attracted him irresistibly and by spring he was back again. He had spent the winter in Madrid where besides painting he published several issues of a magazine "Arte Joven."

In Paris Picasso studied the work of the vanguard, of Gauguin, van Gogh, Toulouse-Lautrec, Vuillard, Denis, and of the older men Degas, Renoir and the Impressionists. During much of 1901 he painted lustily with a rich palette and impressionist brushwork (nos. 9, 10), suddenly, but characteristically, reversing

his style in a series of flat, decorative figure pieces such as the Harlequin (no. 12). He even tried his hand at a poster (no. 14) in the manner of Chéret and Lautrec. In June of 1901 he exhibited a group of canvases at Vollard's and thereby came to know Max Jacob, the poet, who was for years afterwards an intimate and most loyal friend.

4. Heads and figures (Scène de bar): page from a sketchbook. Paris, 1900? Conté crayon, $5\frac{1}{8}$ x $8\frac{1}{4}$ inches. Lent by Walter P. Chrysler, Jr.

5. Le Moulin de la Galette. Paris, 1900(Z). Oil on canvas, $35\frac{1}{4}$ x $45\frac{3}{4}$ inches. Lent by J. Thannhauser. According to the lender, Picasso said recently that this was his first painting done in Paris.

6. Old Musician. 1900? Pencil, $17\frac{1}{8}$ x $11\frac{3}{8}$ inches. Lent by Walter P. Chrysler, Jr.

7

7. Paris Street. Paris, 1900. Oil, 18½ x 26 inches. Lent by Miss Harriet Levy.

8. Two Women and a Hand. 1901? Black and color crayon, 5¼ x 7½ inches. Lent by the Perls Galleries.

9

9. On the Upper Deck. Paris, 1901. Oil, 19⅛ x 25¼ inches. The Art Institute of Chicago, Mr. and Mrs. L. L. Coburn Collection.

The warm color and rich impressionist surface are characteristic of this time in Picasso's development.

11

10. **Bull Ring.** Paris? 1901. Pastel, 7⅛ x 9½ inches. Lent by J. Thannhauser. Related to the oil in the collection of Mrs. Chester Beatty, London (Z. no. 88, pl. 44).

11. **Chrysanthemums.** Paris, 1901? Oil, 32 x 25¾ inches. Lent by Walter P. Chrysler, Jr. Picasso painted a group of flower compositions in 1901 and others in 1904 (Z., pl. 28, 108).

12. **Harlequin.** Paris, 1901 (Z). Oil, 31½ x 23¾ inches. Lent by Mr. and Mrs. Henry Clifford.
For a brief moment before the Blue Period began, Picasso painted in this decorative poster-like manner, possibly under the influence of van Gogh, Maurice Denis and Vuillard.

12

page 27

13

14

13. Burial. Paris, 1901? Pencil and watercolor, 16¾ x 19½ inches. Lent by Walter P. Chrysler, Jr. Apparently related to two similar subjects in oil, Le Mort, and Evocation, both painted in Paris in 1901 (Z., pl. 24, 25). They were among Picasso's first efforts at figure composition in the grand style. This drawing has also been dated 1904.

14. "Jardin Paris": design for a poster. Paris, 1901-02. Watercolor, 25⅛ x 19¼ inches. Lent by Walter P. Chrysler, Jr.

15

Toward the end of 1901 Picasso began to use a pervasive blue tone in his paintings — a tone in harmony with the murky and sometimes heavy-handed pathos of his subject matter — poverty-stricken mothers, wan harlots with femme fatale masks and blind beggars.

15. The Blue Room (Le Tub; Interior with a Bather; Early Morning). Paris, 1901. Oil, 20 x 24½ inches. Lent by the Phillips Memorial Gallery, Washington. Represents Picasso's studio at 130ter, Boulevard Clichy, in 1901. The poster on the wall is by Toulouse Lautrec. (Compare Picasso's own design for a poster, no. 14.) Exhibited with fourteen other works by Picasso at the Galerie Berthe Weill, April, 1902. The Blue Room is one of the first Blue Period canvases.

16

page 30

17

16. Woman with Folded Arms (Elégie). Paris, 1901(Z). Oil, 31⅞ x 23 inches. Lent by Mr. and Mrs. Chauncey McCormick.

17. Mother and Child. Paris, 1901(Z). Oil, 44¼ x 38½ inches. Lent by Maurice Wertheim.

18

18. Two Women at a Bar. Barcelona, 1902(Z). Oil, 31½ x 36 inches. Lent by Walter P. Chrysler, Jr. Formerly
in the collection of Gertrude Stein.

19. La Vie (Couple nu et femme avec enfant). Barcelona, 1903(Z). Oil, 77⅜ x 50⅞ inches. Lent by the Museum
of the Rhode Island School of Design, Providence.

His most ambitious work of the Blue Period is La Vie *of 1903 in which he endows a salon "problem" subject with
serious statuesque dignity (no. 19).*

La Vie, Two Women at a Bar, the Old Guitarist *and many other important works of the Blue Period were done
in Barcelona where Picasso lived much of the time during the years 1902 and 1903 returning to Paris to settle
permanently only at the beginning of 1904. These were "blue" years of poverty and disappointment.*

19

20

22

23

20. The Old Guitarist. Barcelona, 1903(Z). Oil on panel, 47¾ x 32½ inches. The Art Institute of Chicago, Helen Birch Bartlett Memorial Collection.

21. Street Urchins (Les va-nu-pieds; Enfants de la rue). Barcelona, 1903(Z). Color crayon, 14¼ x 10½ inches. Lent by J. Thannhauser.
Reproduced Z., pl. 86.

22. Beggar. 1903? Ink and pencil, 12¼ x 4⅝ inches. Lent by Walter P. Chrysler, Jr.

23. Mother and Child. Paris, 1904(dated). Black crayon, 13½ x 10½ inches. Lent by the Fogg Art Museum, Cambridge, Mass., Paul J. Sachs Collection.

Throughout Picasso's career he has again and again used figure styles which seem closely related to the "mannerist" art of the late 16th century. The elongations, the insistent pathos, the cramped postures or affected gestures of the Old Guitarist (no. 20), the Beggar (no. 22), the Frugal Repast (no. 26) were possibly influenced by the great Spanish mannerists Morales and El Greco.

25

24

24. Woman with a Helmet of Hair (Head of Acrobat's
    Wife). Paris, 1904(dated). Gouache, 16½ x 12 inches.
    Lent by Mr. and Mrs. Walter S. Brewster.

25. Woman with a Crow. Paris, 1904(dated). Gouache
    and pastel, 25½ x 19½ inches. Lent by the Toledo
    Museum of Art.

Early in 1904 the Blue Period came to an end; but for a while the rhetoric, the attenuated hands and mannered poses of 1903 grew even more exaggerated in such works as the perverse Woman with a Crow, the angular and terrible Woman Ironing and the Actor (nos. 25, 27, 29). Then, gradually, these mannerisms gave way to the more natural style and melancholy sweetness of the long series of saltimbanques, acrobats and harlequins of 1905 (nos. 30, 31, 47). Color, too, dispersed the blue gloom of 1903, but it was for the most part subdued and subtle, in harmony with a new delicacy both of drawing and of sentiment.

The poetic charm and repose of this "saltimbanque" period in comparison with the tension of 1902 to 1904 is very probably a reflection of Picasso's own improved circumstances for during 1905 he began to have a moderate success. He was surrounded by brilliant friends, among them Max Jacob, Guillaume Apollinaire (see nos. 41, 50), André Salmon and Gustave Coquiot; and discerning collectors such as the Americans Leo and Gertrude Stein (no. 65) and the Russian Shchukine began to buy his work.

26. The Frugal Repast. 1904. Etching on zinc, 18⅜ x 14⅞ inches; 2nd state, before steel-facing (G. 2, IIa). Lent by Alfred Stieglitz.
    This copy was bought from Picabia and exhibited at Mr. Stieglitz' gallery "291" in 1915.

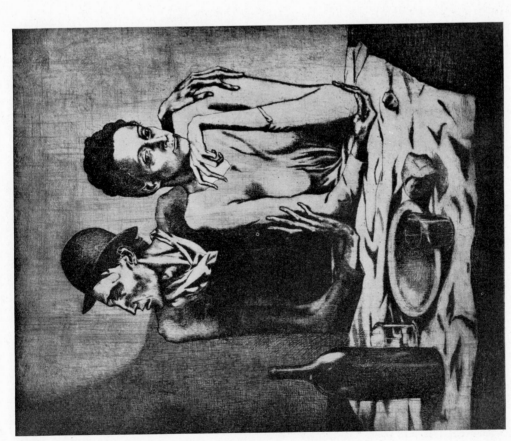

26

27

27. Woman Ironing. Paris, 1904(Z). Oil, 46⅛ x 29⅛ inches. Lent by J. Thannhauser.

28. "Esquisse pour Hôtel de l'Ouest...Chambre 22". Paris, 1904(Z). Watercolor, 21⅜ x 16¾ inches. Lent by Walter P. Chrysler, Jr. Room 22 of the Hôtel de l'Ouest was occupied by Jean Lorrain and Gustave Coquiot in 1904. (Z. no. 213.)

29. The Actor. Paris, winter 1904-05(K). Oil, 77¼ x 45⅛ inches. Lent by Rosenberg and Helft Ltd.

29

30

30. Blue Boy. Paris, 1905(Z). Gouache, 40 x 22½ inches. Lent by Edward M. M. Warburg.

31

31. Two Acrobats with a Dog. Paris, 1905(dated). Gouache, 41½ x 29½ inches. Lent by J. Thannhauser.

32

32. Jester (Tête de Fou). 1905(Z). Bronze, 16¼ inches high. Lent by the Phillips Memorial Gallery, Washington.

In 1905 the dealer Ambroise Vollard cast a series of bronzes modeled by Picasso. This Head of a Jester is related to paintings of actors and clowns of the same year (cf. Zervos pl. 125). Apparently somewhat later are the bronze head and figure (nos. 59, 60). Except for a few isolated, though important, experiments (nos. 83, 115, 119), Picasso was not to take up sculpture seriously again for over twenty years.

39

In 1905 Picasso made a series of some sixteen drypoints and etchings which in their sensitive lyricism epitomize his work of that year. Only a few of each were printed by Delâtre and signed by the artist. Late in 1913 the plates were acquired by Vollard, who steel-faced them and reprinted them, together with the Frugal Repast of 1904, in an edition of 250 copies of each.

33. **The Poor Family.** 1905. Etching on zinc, 9¼ x 7 inches; 2nd state (G. 4, IIb). Lent by Mrs. John D. Rockefeller, Jr.

34. **Bust of a Man.** February 1905. Drypoint, 4¾ x 3½ inches (G. 5b). Lent by Mrs. John D. Rockefeller, Jr.

35. **Two Acrobats.** March 1905. Drypoint, 4¾ x 3 9/16 inches (G. 6b). Lent by Mrs. John D. Rockefeller, Jr.

36. **Head of a Woman in Profile.** 1905. Drypoint, 11½ x 9¾ inches; 1st state (G. 7a). Collection The Museum of Modern Art, New York, Lillie P. Bliss Collection. Compare with the gouache, no. 24.

37. **Acrobats.** 1905. Drypoint, 11¼ x 12⅞ inches (G. 9b). Lent by Mrs. John D. Rockefeller, Jr.

38. **The Watering Place.** 1905. Drypoint, 4¾ x 7 15/16 inches; proof (G. 10a). Lent by Jean Goriany. Compare with the gouache, no. 52.

39. **At the Circus.** 1905. Drypoint, 8⅝ x 5½ inches (G. 11b). Lent by Mrs. John D. Rockefeller, Jr.

43

40. **Clown Resting.** 1905. Drypoint, $4\frac{3}{4}$ x $3\frac{7}{16}$ inches; proof (G. 12a). Lent by Jean Goriany.

41. **The Bath.** 1905. Drypoint, $13\frac{3}{8}$ x $11\frac{1}{4}$ inches; 1st state, early proof, before steel-facing (G. 14a). Lent by the Weyhe Gallery. Inscribed to Guillaume Apollinaire.

42. **The Mother Dressing.** 1905. Etching on zinc, $9\frac{1}{4}$ x $6\frac{7}{8}$ inches (G. 15b). Collection the Art Institute of Chicago.

43. **Salome.** 1905. Drypoint, $15\frac{15}{16}$ x $13\frac{3}{4}$ inches; proof before steel-facing (G. 17a). Lent by the Weyhe Gallery. Inscribed to Monsieur Delâtre, the original publisher of this series of prints.

45

44. The Dance. 1905. Drypoint, 7¼ x 9⅛ inches (G. 18b). Lent by Mrs. John D. Rockefeller, Jr. Compare with the drawing, no. 49.

45. Bust of a Woman. 1905-06. Woodcut, 8⅝ x 5⅜ inches (G. 211). Lent by Jean Goriany. Geiser states that only eight proofs are known.

46. Bust of a Young Woman. 1906. Woodcut, 16½ x 12⅜ inches (G. 212). Lent by the Brooklyn Museum.

47

47. The Harlequin's Family. Paris, 1905 (dated). Gouache, 23 x 17¼ inches. Lent by the Lewisohn Collection.

48

48. Cocks. 1905? Gouache, 8¾ x 9⅝ inches. Lent by Miss Harriet Levy.

49. "Danse barbare." 1905? Ink, 15¾ x 6½ inches. Lent by Miss Harriet Levy. Compare with the drypoint, The Dance of 1905, no. 44, and the drawing, La belle qui passe (Stein, bibl. 206 Eng. ed., pl. 54).

50. "EX-LIBRIS: Guillaume Apollinaire." Paris, 1905(Z). Ink and watercolor, 7½ x 4¾ inches. Lent by Walter P. Chrysler, Jr. Reproduced Z., pl. 100. Apollinaire was later to be the brilliant champion of cubism.

51. La Coiffure. Paris, 1905(Z). Oil, 68⅞ x 39¼ inches. Collection the Museum of Modern Art New York. Reproduced Z., pl. 41

A visit to Holland in the summer of 1905 marked a further advance toward a more objective mood in Picasso's art and toward forms of greater weight and monumentality, a direction which he followed consistently through the Rose Period of 1905-06 almost to the time of the Demoiselles d'Avignon *painted a year later.*

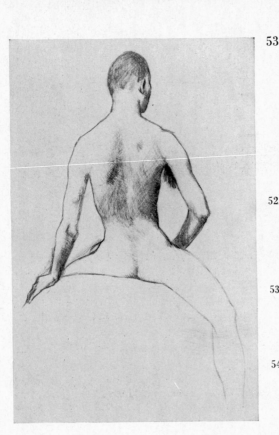

52

53

52. The Watering Place (Chevaux au bain; L'abreu-voir). Paris, 1905(Z). Gouache, 14⅞ x 23 inches. Lent anonymously, courtesy the Worcester Art Museum. A study presumably for a large scale composition. Compare the drawing, no. 53, the large painting, no. 54, and the etching, no. 38.

53. Youth on Horseback. Paris, 1905. Charcoal, 18⅜ x 12 inches. Lent by John W. Warrington. Study for a composition of men and horses of which the gouache, no. 52, is the most complete version. (Compare Z., pl. 118.)

54. Boy Leading a Horse (Le meneur de cheval). Paris, 1905(Z). Oil, 86½ x 51¼ inches. Lent by William S. Paley. A similar group occurs in the center of the composition, The Watering Place, no. 52.

54

page 49

55

55. Woman with a Fan (Femme au bras levé). Paris, 1905(dated). Oil, 39½ x 32 inches. Lent by Mr. and Mrs. William Averell Harriman.

56

56. Woman with Loaves. Gosol, 1905 (dated). Oil, 39 x 27½ inches. Lent by the Philadelphia Museum of Art.

57

57. **La Toilette.   Gosol, 1905 (Z). Oil, 59½ x 39½ inches. Lent by the Buffalo Fine Arts Academy,
Albright Art Gallery, Buffalo.**

page 52

58

58. Fernande Olivier. Paris, 1905(Z) or Gosol, summer 1906(K). Oil, 39⅜ x 31⅞
inches. Lent anonymously.

THE ROSE PERIOD. *At Gosol in the Andorra valley of the Spanish Pyrenees, Picasso*
passed some weeks late in 1905 and again in 1906. During this time he left behind him
the nostalgic introspective mood and the emaciated forms of the harlequins of the previ-
ous year. Without at first sacrificing charm, he began to paint figures of an impersonal
placid dignity. He turned too from the superb color of the Woman with a Fan, *no. 55, to*
a chalky terra cotta pink tonality only a little less pervasive than the monochrome of the
Blue Period. The serenity, the graciousness of such early Rose Period paintings as
La Toilette *seem directly inspired by Greek art but the classicism evident here is more*
natural and informal than that of the highly sophisticated Greco-Roman figures of
Picasso's post-War period.

62

62. Head with a Kerchief. Gosol, 1905(Z). Gouache, 24 x 18 inches. Lent by T. Catesby Jones.

The gradual change from an easy natural style to an almost archaic stiffness can be seen by comparing the gouache, no. 61, with the drawing, no. 63.

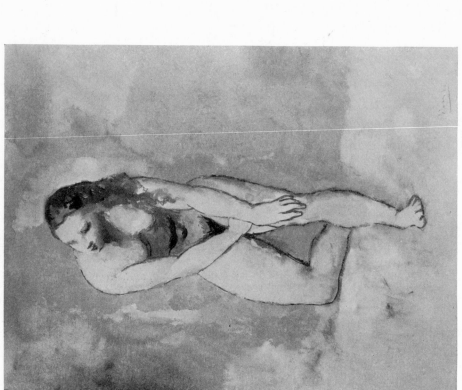

61

59. Woman's Head. Paris, 1905(Z). Bronze, 14 inches high. Lent by the Weyhe Gallery. Reproduced Z., pl. 149.

60. Woman Combing Her Hair. Paris, 1905(Z). Bronze 16½ inches high. Lent by Walter P. Chrysler, Jr., courtesy the Buchholz Gallery. Reproduced Z., pl. 153.

61. Standing Nude. Gosol, 1905(Z). Gouache, 25¼ x 19¼ inches. Lent by the Cleveland Museum of Art, Hinman B. Hurlbut Collection. A study for the oil, Harem, in the collection of Leonard C. Hanna, Jr., Z., pl. 147.

64

64. Figure Study, Back. 1906. Charcoal, 24½ x 18½ inches. Lent by Walter P. Chrysler, Jr.

63

63. Peasants from Andorra. Gosol, 1906. Ink, 22⅞ x 13½ inches. Collection the Art Institute of Chicago, gift of Robert Allerton.

65

65. Gertrude Stein.   Paris, 1906(Z). Oil. Lent by Miss Gertrude Stein.

This monumental portrait, one of Picasso's most renowned works, and the Self Portrait, *oppo-*
site, reveal the vigorous sculptural forms and mask-like faces which Picasso developed in 1906
toward the end of the Rose Period. Gertrude Stein was one of Picasso's chief patrons at this
time and was later to write extensively about him (see bibl. 203-06).

66

66. Self Portrait.   Paris, 1906(dated). Oil, 36 x 28 inches. Lent by the Museum of Living
    Art, New York University. Another characteristic work of this moment is the woodcut,
    no. 46.

67

67. **Two Nudes.**   Paris, 1906(Z). Oil, 59¾ x 36⅝ inches. Lent by Rosenberg and Helft Ltd.

THE "NEGRO" PERIOD
THE BEGINNING OF CUBISM

On October 25th, 1906, Picasso was twenty-five years old. During the previous five years he had produced over two hundred paintings and many hundreds of drawings, an output in quantity and quality such as few painters accomplish in a lifetime. But the Blue Period with its belated fin-de-siècle desperation, the wistful acrobats of 1905, the tranquil classicism of the Rose Period, all this cumulative achievement was, so far as the main highway of modern painting was concerned, a personal and private bypath.

But towards the end of 1906 Picasso changed the direction of his art and in so doing helped change to a remarkable extent the character of modern art as a whole. Cubism, the name subsequently given to this new direction, was not Picasso's single-handed invention; it was in fact something of a collaborative venture to which Braque among others contributed importantly; it was nourished, too, in various ways by Cézanne, Henri Rousseau, Seurat, Negro sculpture, the critic Apollinaire, the dealer Kahnweiler. But it was above all the quality and power of Picasso's art that made cubism the characteristic movement in the art of the first quarter of our century.

THE AUTUMN SALON OF 1905

In 1905, a year before, while Picasso was engaged in his soliloquy with harlequins, two events of great historic importance occurred at the Autumn Salon. The most conspicuous of these was the first exhibition of a group of young painters which a critic in derision called les fauves, the wild beasts. Braque, Friesz, Derain were among them and Matisse was their leader. The fauves seemed revolutionary because they had gone beyond Gauguin and van Gogh in their use of heavy distorted outlines and bold flat patterns of arbitrary color. Back of these violent innovations lay the idea that painting should be primarily an expression of pure esthetic experience and that the enjoyment of line and form and color was a sufficient end in itself. The representation of natural forms therefore seemed more or less irrelevant, though some resemblance to nature as a point of departure was not excluded. This emphatic declaration of art's independence of nature was an important factor in the background of cubism. The fauves had also looked to exotic and primitive arts for sanction and inspiration and it was through them that Picasso came

at this time under the influence of African Negro sculpture, the first of many non-European traditions which were to interest him in the course of his career.

The other significant event at the Autumn Salon of 1905 was a section of ten paintings by Cézanne whose importance had been obscured in the eyes of the young avant-garde by the more obvious and facile innovations of Gauguin and van Gogh. Ten more Cézannes were shown in 1906, the year he died, and fifty-six at a memorial exhibition in 1907. For about five years, from the end of 1906 on, the profound and difficult art of Cézanne exerted a strong influence upon Picasso.

Little affected at first by these events, Picasso's own art prior to the end of 1906 had passed, on the plane of sentiment, from the near-bathos of the Blue Period through the gentle melancholy of the saltimbanques and the ingratiating detachment of the Rose figures to the comparatively impersonal masks of the Gertrude Stein and self portraits; and in figure style this change had been paralleled since 1904 by an ever increasing sculptural solidity of form. The Two Nudes, illustrated on the opposite page, painted late in 1906, are the logical conclusion of these two tendencies. Already influenced perhaps by the squat proportions of West African sculpture, these massive figures seem an emphatic expression of Picasso's denial both of sentiment and of traditional or conventional beauty; positively the Two Nudes are an assertion of his growing interest in objective esthetic problems, in this case the creation of volumes and masses and their composition within the painted space of the picture. It is instructive to turn back to earlier two-figure compositions, the Harlequin Family (no. 47) and later La Toilette (no. 57). The Two Nudes is the end of the series.

LES DEMOISELLES D'AVIGNON

What happened next in Picasso's art is concentrated in one extraordinary picture, the Demoiselles d'Avignon, begun toward the end of 1906 and finished in 1907 after months of development and revision (no. 71). As the first of the three studies (no. 68) suggests, the composition of the Demoiselles is probably inspired by one of Cézanne's late bather pictures in which the figures and background are fused in a kind of relief without much indication either of deep space or of weight in the forms. It is also possible that memories of El Greco's compact figure compositions and the angular highlights of his draperies, rocks and skies may have

68

69

70

confirmed the suggestions drawn from Cézanne. More conspicuous is the archaic schematic drawing possibly under the influence of Negro sculpture. The masks of the figures at the right are more directly derived from Negro art of the Ivory Coast or French Congo and surpass in their barbaric intensity the most vehement inventions of les fauves. (See Goldwater, bibl. 100).

The Demoiselles d'Avignon is the masterpiece of Picasso's Negro Period, but it may also be called the first cubist picture, for the breaking up of natural forms, whether figures, still life or drapery, into a semiabstract all-over pattern of tilting shifting planes is already cubism; cubism in a rudimentary stage, it is true, but closer to the developed cubism of 1909 than are most of the intervening "Negro" works. The Demoiselles is a transitional picture, a laboratory or, better, a battlefield of trial and experiment; but it is also a work of formidable, dynamic power unsurpassed in European art of its time. Together with Matisse's Joie de Vivre of the same year it marks the beginning of a new period in the history of modern art.

68. Composition study for Les Demoiselles d'Avignon. 1907(dated on back). Charcoal and pastel, 18⅞ x 25 inches. Lent by the artist. An early study with seven figures — five female nudes and two clothed male figures. The figure at the left, Picasso says (1939), is a man with a skull in his hand entering a scene of carnal pleasure. The three figures at the right and the melons reappear in the final painting.

69. Composition study for Les Demoiselles d'Avignon. Paris, 1907. Oil on wood, 7⅜ x 9⅜ inches. Lent by the artist. A slightly later study than no. 68; still with seven figures but the central seated male figure has given place to a female nude.

70. Composition study for Les Demoiselles d'Avignon. 1907(dated). Watercolor, 6¾ x 8¾ inches. Lent by the Museum of Living Art, New York University. A late study with five female figures. The man entering at the left of the earlier studies, nos. 68 and 69, has been changed into a female figure pulling back the curtain, related to the left-hand figure of Two Nudes, no. 67, but more directly borrowed from an earlier composition of 1906(Z., pl. 165, 166). All implications of a moralistic contrast between virtue (the man with a skull) and vice (the man surrounded by food and women) have been eliminated in favor of a purely formal figure composition, which as it develops becomes more and more compact, angular, and abstract.

71

71. Les Demoiselles d'Avignon. Paris, 1906-07. Oil, 96 x 92 inches. Collection the Museum of Modern Art, New York, acquired through the Lillie P. Bliss Bequest.

page 61

72

72. Dancer (Grande danseuse d'Avignon; Danseuse nègre). Avignon? 1907(P). Oil,
59 x 39¼ inches. Lent by Walter P. Chrysler, Jr.

More completely under the influence of African art, particularly of the metal-covered
grave figures of the Gabun, than are the right-hand figures of Les Demoiselles d'Avignon.
The very flat handling and dramatic movement are characteristic of only a brief
moment in the "Negro" Period.

76

75

73. Dancer. 1907(P). Watercolor, 25¾ x 19½ inches. Lent by Walter P. Chrysler, Jr. A study for the Dancer, no. 72. Also related to the right-hand background figure in Les Demoiselles d'Avignon, no. 71.

74. Standing Figure. 1907(P). Brush and ink, 11½ x 7¼ inches. Lent by Walter P. Chrysler, Jr. Possibly a study for the central figure of Les Demoiselles d'Avignon.

75. Figure Turned to the Left. 1907. Woodcut, $8\frac{9}{16}$ x 5⅜ inches (G. 218). Lent by Jean Goriany. Geiser states that there is but one proof, yet this is clearly a second proof differing from the one he reproduces and describes as unique. Related to the left central figure of Les Demoiselles d'Avignon, no. 71.

76. Head (Femme au nez en quart de Brie). 1907? (dated on stretcher October, 1905, but the style is apparently of two years later). Oil, 13⅞ x 10¾ inches. Lent by Roland Penrose.

77

77. Woman in Yellow (Le corsage jaune). 1907(P). Oil, 51¼ x 37⅞ inches. Lent by Mr. and
Mrs. Joseph Pulitzer, Jr.

78

78. Head (Tête nègre). Summer 1908(K). Oil, 24½ x 17 inches. Lent by Walter P. Chrysler, Jr.

By the middle of 1908 Picasso had passed through the barbaric phase of his Negro Period and was painting soberly impressive studies of heads (no. 78) and still life (no. 79) using a brown red monochrome. In contrast to the flat patterns of 1907, both perspective and modeling are used to give a simple three-dimensional sculptural effect.

It is worth recording that Picasso at the present time is particularly interested in the work of this Negro Period. Fortunately the Demoiselles d'Avignon, *no. 71, the* Dancer, *no. 72, and the* Woman in Yellow, *opposite, the three most important works of the period west of Moscow, can be included in the exhibition. The Museum of Modern Western Art in Moscow has several other important "Negro" Picassos originally bought by Shchukine.*

79

79. Bowls and Jug. Paris, summer 1908(K).
Oil, 32 x 25½ inches. Lent by the Museum of
Living Art, New York University. The same
period as the Head, no. 78.

80. Landscape with Figures. Paris, autumn
1908(K). Oil, 23⅝ x 28¾ inches. Lent by the
artist. Related in style to the two previous
pictures. Unfortunately the series of landscapes done at Horta in the succeeding year
cannot be represented in the exhibition.

81. Figures in a Landscape. Autumn 1908(K).
Gouache, 18¾ x 23⅛ inches. Lent by Mr.
and Mrs. Samuel S. White 3rd.

80

82

82. Fruit Dish. Spring 1909(K). Oil, 28¾ x 23⅜ inches. Lent by the Bignou Gallery.

ANALYTICAL CUBISM

With a series of greenish paintings begun early in 1909 Picasso continued his progress toward a more developed and abstract form of cubism, a progress which had been interrupted by the simplified brown paintings of the end of the Negro Period (nos. 78 and 79). The forms in the Fruit Dish are more complicated than in the Bowls and Jug of the previous year; perspective, foreshortening and modeling are abbreviated so that suggestions of space and weight are diminished. The tilted table top of Cézanne's late still life style is recalled and exaggerated.

Analytical cubism — cubism which "analyzes," breaks up, takes apart natural forms — is a term frequently applied to cubist painting of 1909 to 1912-13, particularly the work of Picasso and Braque.

84

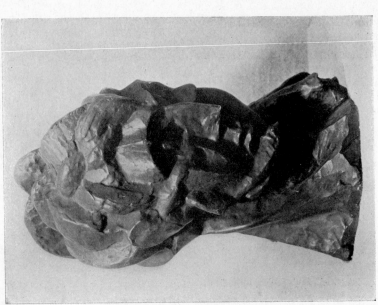

83

83. Woman's Head. 1909? Bronze, 16¼ inches high. Lent
by the Weyhe Gallery.

An isolated piece in Picasso's sculpture but closely related
to his paintings of the period such as the Woman with
Pears which shows the same breaking up of surfaces into
angular facets without as yet destroying the underlying
sculptural form.

84. Woman with Pears. 1909(K). Oil, 36 x 28¾ inches. Lent by Walter P. Chrysler, Jr. Sometimes dated 1908.

85. Two Nudes. 1909. Drypoint, 5⅛ x 4⅜ inches; 3rd state (G. 21, IIIb). Lent by Jean Goriany.

86. Still Life. 1909. Drypoint, 5⅛ x 4⅜ inches; 3rd state (G. 22, IIIb.) Lent by Jean Goriany.

87. Head. 1909. Gouache, 24½ x 18½ inches. Lent by Walter P. Chrysler, Jr.

88. Woman's Head. 1909(K). Gouache, 24 x 18 inches. Collection the Museum of Modern Art, New York, gift of Mrs. Saidie A. May.

89. Portrait of Braque. Late 1909(K). Oil, 24¾ x 19¾ inches. Lent by Frank Crowninshield.

Georges Braque, Picasso's partner in cubism, had been a member of the fauves group in 1905. By 1909 he was working so closely with Picasso that it is hard in some cases to distinguish their work. Braque reaffirmed the importance of Cézanne to cubism and, later, it is said anticipated Picasso in using trompe l'oeil (fool the eye) perspective, imitation textures and letters as elements in cubism.

The Portrait of Braque marks a step beyond the Woman with Pears in the cubist disintegration of natural forms. In this and the following paintings color gives way to a tan greyish monochrome.

The term "cubism" is said to have been derived from a disparaging remark made by Matisse about "les petits cubes" while looking at some Braque landscapes of 1908. Actually the "cubes" of Braque's and Picasso's cubism were to flatten out and virtually disappear within a year or two afterwards. In 1911 Guillaume Apollinaire, spokesman for the movement, adopted the term "cubism" officially.

89

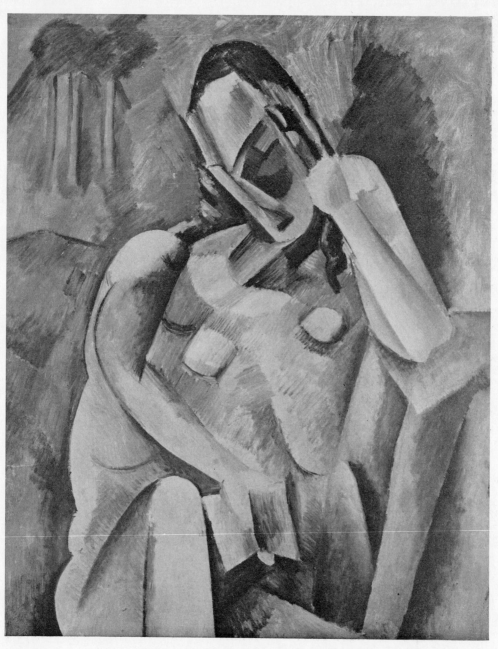

90

90. Woman in a Landscape. Late 1909(K). Oil, 36¼ x 28½ inches. Lent by Walter P. Chrysler, Jr.

91

91. Woman with a Mandolin. 1910(dated). Oil, 39½ x 29 inches. Lent by Roland Penrose.

More geometrical in character than the Woman in a Landscape; *the deformations are more radical, but still with a good deal of sculptural modeling.*

Although cubism seems primarily concerned with formal esthetics, its fantastic aspects and psychological implications have won it honor among the post-War Surrealists.

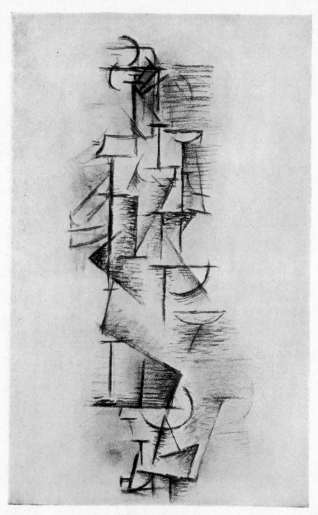

92

92. Figure. 1910. Charcoal, 19 x 12¼ inches. Lent by Alfred Stieglitz. Included in a retrospective exhibition of 83 Picasso drawings and etchings at Mr. Stieglitz' gallery "291," April 1911, the first one-man Picasso show in America (see list of Picasso exhibitions, page 199) and probably the first time Picasso was exhibited in any way in this country.

93. Four etchings for the book Saint-Matorel by Max Jacob. 1910(G.23-26). Published by Kahnweiler, Paris, 1911. Lent by Pierre Loeb.

94. Standing Figure. 1910? Oil. Lent by Mrs. Meric
     Callery. Also dated 1911 and 1912.

94

*Cubism grew rapidly more abstract in 1910. Sculptural
or modeled forms and continuous contours were eliminated in favor of flattish quasi-geometrical planes and
broken silhouettes. The curved lines in the drawing,
no. 92, and the painting, no. 94, suggest cross-sections
of the figure. The planes are subtly graded in tone so
that they seem to tilt forward or back and at times to
merge with the background space. In these works and
those reproduced on the following three pages, cubism
passed through its most austere period. Picasso and
Braque analyzed, simplified, geometrized the forms of
nature, transmuting them with an ascetic, uncompro-
mising discipline. These works are not entirely "abstract," they retain certain vestiges of the "model" but
these very vestiges serve to indicate the process of
abstraction and lead to a more complicated esthetic
tension than is possible in purely abstract compositions
of squares or circles.*

95

95. Nude. Cadaqués, 1910? Oil, 38¾ x 30½ inches. Lent by Mr. and Mrs. Walter C. Arensberg. Also
    dated 1911, but compare one of the Saint-Matorel etchings, Mlle. Léonie dans une chaise longue,
    G. 25, state III, dated 1910.

96

96. Portrait of Kahnweiler.   Autumn 1910(K). Oil, 39¼ x 28¼ inches. Lent by Mrs. Charles B. Goodspeed.

In certain portraits of 1910 Picasso used a more methodical and complex system of disintegration than in the Nude, opposite, or the Figure, no. 94. Henry Kahnweiler was an enthusiastic dealer who from about 1907 to 1914 was one of the chief champions of cubism. He remains one of its soundest historians (see bibl. no. 121 and chronology, page 21).

97

97. Pierrot (Seated Man; Accordionist). Céret, summer 1911(K). Oil, 51¼ x 35⅛ inches. Lent by the Solomon R. Guggenheim Foundation, New York.

At Céret in the Pyrenees Picasso and Braque spent the summer of 1911 working together almost in collaboration.

100

98. **Girl and Soldier.** Paris, spring 1912(K). Oil, 47½ x 33 inches. Lent by Pierre Loeb. Reproduced bibl. 228, p. 213.

99. **"Ma Jolie"** (Woman with a Guitar). Paris, spring 1912(K). Oil, 39⅜ x 25¾ inches. Lent by Marcel Fleischmann. Reproduced bibl. 38, p. 110.

100. **L'Arlésienne.** Sorgues, summer 1912(K). Also dated 1910 and 1911. Oil, 28¾ x 21¼ inches. Lent by Walter P. Chrysler, Jr.

In the head may be seen the cubist device of simultaneity — showing two aspects of a single object at the same time, in this case the profile and full face. The transparency of overlapping planes is also characteristic. These devices have been used by Picasso in many later periods, including the recent "double-faced" portraits Compare nos. 165, 175, 189, 208, 249, 349.

101. **Head of a Man.** 1912. Etching, 5⅛ x 4⁵⁄₁₆ inches (G. 32b). Lent by Mrs. John D. Rockefeller, Jr.

102. **Still Life with Bottle.** 1912. Drypoint, 19¾ x 12 inches (G. 33b). Lent by the Weyhe Gallery. Picasso's most important cubist print.

104. Guitar. 1912(P). Charcoal, 24⅜ x 18⅜ inches. Lent by Rosenberg and Helft, Ltd.

105. Man with a Hat. Paris, winter 1913(K). Pasted paper, charcoal and ink, 24½ x 18¼ inches. Collection the Museum of Modern Art, New York.

104

103. Still Life with Chair Caning. 1911-12. Oil and pasted paper simulating chair caning, on canvas, oval 10⅝ x 13¾ inches. Lent by the artist, who suggests that this may be dated 1911 and is the first papier collé (composition with pasted paper). However, other small oval still lifes of this type are dated 1912.

In this small oval are concentrated three cubist innovations of 1911-12: the introduction of letters, of pasted paper (papier collé), and of trompe l'oeil imitation textures. In this case simulated texture and pasted paper are combined, for the chair caning is actually a piece of wall paper. These techniques, most of them introduced by Braque, added complexity and variety to cubism but also marked the beginning of its decline from the ascetic purity of such works as the Figure, no. 94, or the Seated Man, no. 97.

Some of the papier collés of 1912-13 are, however, among the most exacting and precisely calculated of Picasso's works (nos. 105-107).

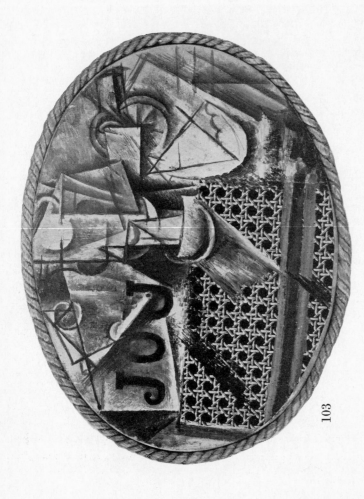

103

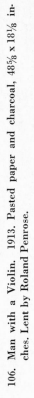

107

106. **Man with a Violin.** 1913. Pasted paper and charcoal, 48⅝ x 18⅛ inches. Lent by Roland Penrose.

107. **Still Life.** 1913. Pasted paper and charcoal, 24¼ x 18½ inches. Lent by Alfred Stieglitz. First exhibited in America at Gallery "291," 1915.

106

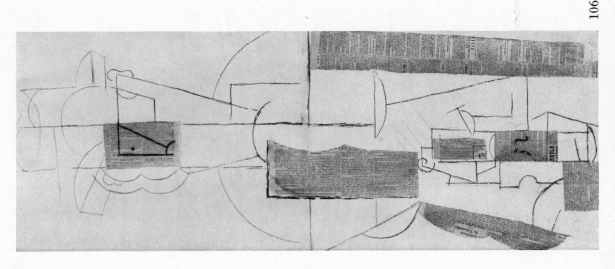

108

108. Portrait with the words "J'aime Eva." 1912 (dated on back). Oil, 38¾ x 25 inches. Lent by the Columbus Gallery of Fine Arts, Ferdinand Howald Collection.

This painting, the drawing, no. 104, the pasted paper, no. 107, illustrate the transition from analytical to synthetic cubism, in which the analysis or fragmentation of natural forms is supplemented by invented quasi-geometrical forms used in free combination with certain vestiges of the original object. Cubism after 1912 is comparatively synthetic or subjective as opposed to analytical or objective. This resulted on the whole in simpler compositions with fewer details.

109

109. The Model. 1912(K) or 1913. Oil, 45½ x 31½ inches. Lent by Walter P. Chrysler, Jr.

The enrichment of cubist technique by a variety of simulated textures, a thicker impasto, and the tentative beginning of a return to color are all apparent in this painting.

110. Head. 1912-13. Charcoal, 24 x 18⅜ inches. Lent anonymously.

111

Cubist interest in textures increases during 1913-14 in such complex arrangements as this still life and the oval composition opposite in which a variety of paper and painted surfaces is combined in compositions of predominantly rectangular shapes. The result is not merely a surface enrichment but an emphasis upon the sensuous tactile reality of the surface itself in contrast to painting in the past which through more or less realistic methods took the eye and mind past the surface of the canvas to represented objects such as figures or landscapes. Yet though it almost eliminated the realistic form of the symbol, cubism did not do away with the symbol entirely. The ever-recurring guitars, violins, bottles, playing cards, pipes, cigarettes, and the fragmentary words referring to newspapers, music and beverages constitute a fairly consistent "subject matter" or iconography, which may have more than incidental significance as references to "artificial objects of private manipulation." (See Shapiro, Nature of abstract art. Marxist Quarterly, v. 1, 1937, p. 93.)

111. **Still Life with a Guitar.** Paris, spring 1913 (dated on back). Oil and pasted paper, 25⅝ x 21⅛ inches. Lent by Sidney Janis.

112. **Still Life with Fruit.** Paris, winter 1913 (K). Pasted paper and charcoal, 25½ x 19½ inches. Lent by the Museum of Living Art, New York University. Reproduced Museum of Living Art, A. E. Gallatin Collection, New York University, 1936, pl. 105.

113. **Still Life.** 1913? Oil. Collection Mr. and Mrs. Walter C. Arensberg.

113

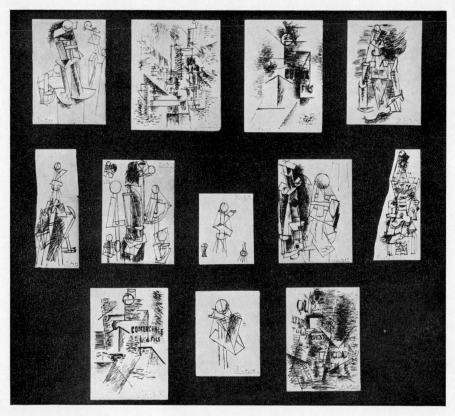

114

114. Twelve Cubist Studies. 1912?-13. Ink, about 5 to 7 inches high. Lent by Pierre Loeb.

Some of these drawings are of considerable interest because by means of perspective they represent constructions in three dimensions in contrast to the flat almost spaceless cubist compositions usual in this period. These perspective drawings are doubtless related to the relief constructions of 1913-14 in wood and other materials like that illustrated. They mark one more step in the growing range of cubist esthetics.

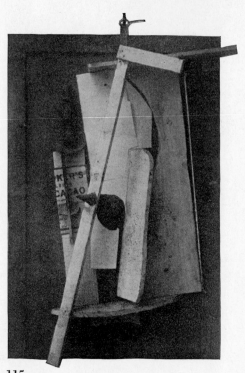

115

115. Relief Construction: Guitar. 1913. Wood and pasted paper. (Not in exhibition.)

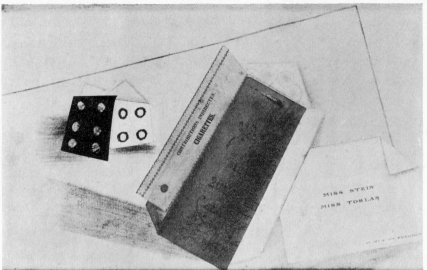

116

117

116. Still Life with a Calling Card (The Package of Cigarettes). 1914(K). Pasted paper and crayon, 5½ x 8¼ inches. Lent by Mrs. Charles B. Goodspeed.

Anti-"literary" in their art, the cubists paradoxically painted letters. Sometimes the letters seem chosen at random but often, as has been mentioned, they refer to drinks or newspapers, and sometimes to people, almost in the manner of literary dedications as in the above papier collé *or in the paintings, nos. 99, 108.*

117. Head. 1914(K); also dated 1913. Pasted paper and charcoal, 17⅛ x 13⅛ inches. Lent by Roland Penrose. One of the most arbitrary and abstract of Picasso's cubist compositions in its remoteness from the object indicated by the title. Particularly admired by the Surrealists.

118

118. Bird on a Branch. Céret, summer 1913 (K). Oil, 13 x 5⅞ inches. Lent anonymously.

In 1914 Picasso's cubism underwent a rapid and radical change from the severe geometrical forms of the previous years to soft irregular shapes peppered with confetti-like dots borrowed from the neo-impressionist technique of Seurat. The change in color from greys, tans, and blacks to brilliant greens and gay reds contributes to a sense of relaxation and even a certain rococo triviality after years of rigorous discipline.

119. Glass of Absinthe. 1914. Painted bronze, 8¾ inches high. Lent by the Museum of Living Art, New York University. Six casts were made for Kahnweiler, each one differently painted. The glass is similar to that in the painting "Vive la," illustrated opposite.

119a. Picasso and Derain: Four still lifes. Avignon, 1914. Painted tile, 21¼ x 21¼ inches. Divided into quarters of which the left-hand two are by Picasso, right-hand two by Derain. Lent by the Buchholz Gallery.

119

122

120. Green Still Life. 1914(dated). Oil, 23½ x 31¼ inches. The Museum of Modern Art, New York, Lillie P. Bliss Collection.

121. Three etchings and drypoints for the book, Le Siège de Jérusalem by Max Jacob (G. 35-37). Paris, Kahnweiler, 1914. Lent by Monroe Wheeler.

122. Still Life: "Vive la . . ." Avignon, 1914; Paris, 1915 (dated on back). Oil, 21⅜ x 25¾ inches. Lent by Sidney Janis.

123. Man with a Guitar. 1915. Engraving with burin on copper, 5¾ x 4¼ inches; 9th state (G. 51, IX). Lent by Jean Goriany.

124. Head(P). 1917(K). Oil on panel, 9¼ x 7¼ inches. Lent by George L. K. Morris. Illustrated out of chronological order, though it seems closely related to certain etchings of 1915 (compare G. 42). Picasso's title emphasizes the high degree of abstraction attained in many works of the period 1915-18.

124

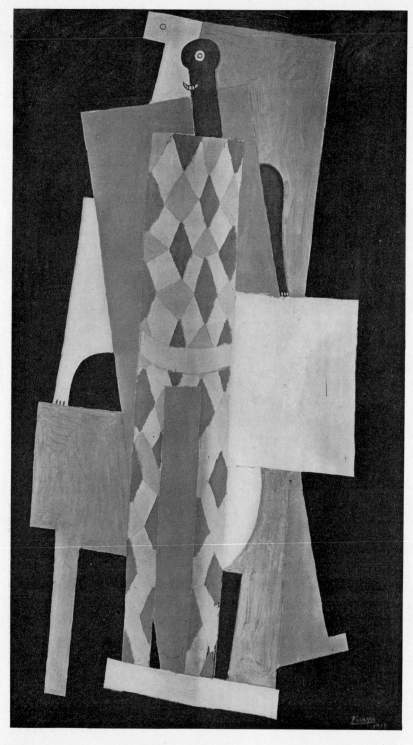

126

125. Fireplace with a Guitar.   1915 (dated). Oil, 51¼ x 37⅞ inches. Lent by Pierre Loeb.

126. Harlequin.   1915 (dated). Oil, 71¼ x 41⅜ inches. Lent anonymously.

The soft rococo style of the still lifes, nos. 119, 120, 122, lasted but a few months. By the end of 1915 Picasso was working in a monumental rectangular cubist style with comparatively large planes usually strong in color and often embellished with pointillist dots.

During 1915, however, he also began a re-return to realism in a series of portrait drawings.

127

127. The Fireplace. 1916-17. Oil, 58⅛ x 26½ inches. Lent by Mr. and Mrs. Joseph Pulitzer, Jr.

128. Guitar. 1916-17. Oil, charcoal and pinned paper, 85 x 31 inches. Lent by A. Conger Good-year.

Bold rectangular design is characteristic of these years of synthetic cubism which come to a climax in the Three Musicians of 1921, nos. 164, 165. Another painting of 1917 is no. 124.

128

129

129. Chinese Conjurer's Costume (Le Chinois). Rome? 1917. Gouache, 10¾ x 7⅜ inches. Lent anonymously. Costume design for the ballet Parade (see p. 192). Massine wore this costume in the original production.

130. Diaghilev and Selisburg. Rome or Florence, 1917. Pencil, 24⅞ x 18⅞ inches. Lent by the artist.

Early in 1917 Picasso went with Jean Cocteau to Rome and Florence to join the Diaghilev Ballet for which he then designed the costumes of Parade. *This portrait of the great impresario is one of a long series of Ingres-like drawings begun in 1915, and including ultimately portraits of Apollinaire, Satie, Massine, Stravinsky, Valéry, Breton, Cocteau, Reverdy, Eluard, Radiguet, Paul Rosenberg, Claribel Cone and others. Mr. Selisburg, the seated figure, was Mr. Otto Kahn's lawyer.*

130

RETURN TO "REALISM";
THE "CLASSIC" PERIOD; THE BALLET.

The portrait drawings of 1915 have been mentioned as the first intimation of a new "realistic" or "classic" style. For ten years afterwards this style was to run in a kind of rivalry with cubism in Picasso's paintings and even down to the present time in prints and illustrated books. Picasso's classic style, inspired at first by the drawings of Ingres, was greatly stimulated during the years 1917 to 1925 by the Russian Ballet which aroused in him a renewed interest in the natural and esthetic beauty of the human body — an interest which he had already shown during his first classic period in 1905-06 (nos. 57, 43).

BALLETS IN WHICH
PICASSO COLLABORATED:

Parade, 1917; Le Tricorne, 1919; Pulcinella, 1920; Cuadro Flamenco, 1921; Mercure, 1924; and Le Train Bleu, 1924.

A more detailed catalog of the Diaghilev ballets for which Picasso designed settings and costumes is given on page 192.

132

132. Three Ballerinas. 1917? Pencil and charcoal, 23⅛ x 17⅞ inches.
Lent by the artist.

131

131. Head of Pierrot. 1917 (dated). Ink, 23½ x 19 inches. Lent by John
W. Warrington. Apparently a study for the painting, no. 139.

134

134. **Pierrot and Harlequin.** 1919. Gouache, 10⅛ x 7¾ inches. Lent by Mrs. Charles B. Goodspeed. Said to be a costume design for the ballet Le Tricorne (see p. 192).

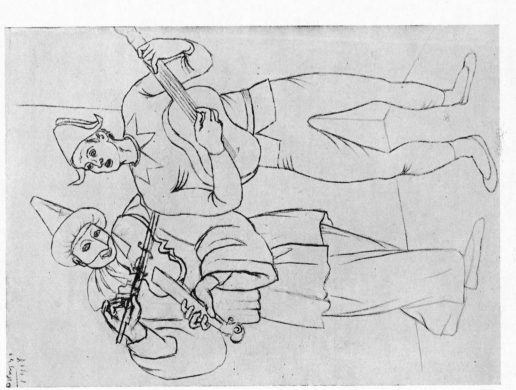

133

133. **Pierrot and Harlequin.** 1918 (dated). Pencil, 10¼ x 7½ inches. Lent by Mrs. Charles B. Goodspeed. Said to be a costume study for the ballet Pulcinella, produced in 1920 (see p. 192); the drawing, however, is dated 1918. Compare with the cubist Pierrot and Harlequin, adjacent.

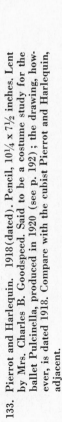

135

136

135. Study for the curtain of the ballet, Le Tricorne, 2nd version. 1919. Oil, 14¾ x 18 inches. Lent anonymously. Inscribed: "A mon cher Paul Rosenberg son ami Picasso" (see p. 192).

136. Costume Design. 1919? Gouache, 6 x 4 inches. Lent by Mrs. Ray Slater Murphy. The artist informed the owner that this is a design for a ballet costume; it seems related to the designs for Le Tricorne.

137. Harlequin. 1919-20? Gouache, 13 x 9½ inches. Lent by Miss Edith Wetmore. Possibly related to the costume designs for the ballet, Pulcinella, 1920.

The original designs for ballet costumes and settings, and the drawings related to the ballet, nos. 129-137, and the section of décor for Cuadro Flamenco, no. 138, opposite, are grouped for convenience on these and the previous pages even though this arrangement breaks the chronological order. The gouache, The Race, no. 167, later used as the design for the curtain of Le Train Bleu, is illustrated in the color frontispiece. In the exhibition are other items, especially illustrated programs, relating to Picasso's work for the ballet. A later series of drawings inspired by the ballet is represented by nos. 194 to 197 of 1925.

138

138. The Theatre Box. 1921. Oil, 76½ x 58⅜ inches. Lent by Rosenberg and Helft, Ltd. A section cut from the scenery of the ballet, Cuadro Flamenco (see p. 192).

139

139. Pierrot Seated. 1918(dated). Oil, 36½ x 28¾ inches. Lent by the Lewisohn Collection.

The parallel course of Picasso's cubist and "realistic" styles is illustrated by comparing this Pierrot *and the* harlequin Violinist, *opposite, both done during the same year.*

140

140. The Violinist ("Si tu veux"). 1918(dated). Oil, 56 x 39½ inches. Lent anonymously.

141. Still Life with a Pipe. 1918(dated). Oil, 8⅝ x 10½ inches. Lent anonymously.

142

page 98

144

142. Bathers. 1918 (dated). Pencil, 9⅛ x 12¼ inches. Lent by the Fogg Art Museum, Cambridge, Mass., Paul J. Sachs Collection.

143. Philosopher. 1918? Pencil, 13⅝ x 10⅞ inches. Lent by the Fogg Art Museum, Cambridge, Mass., Paul J. Sachs Collection. The sitter is said to be a Russian singer.

144. Fisherman. 1918 (dated). Pencil, 13¾ x 10 inches. Lent anonymously.

These three drawings are among the finest of Picasso's "classic" period; and the Bathers is one of the most elaborate of all Picasso's figure compositions. The distortions and elegant simplifications are obviously influenced by the art of Ingres. (The reproductions of the Bathers and the Fisherman were treated with asphaltum during the engraving process, making the line coarser and darker than in the originals which are so exquisitely delicate that they would almost have disappeared in an ordinary half-tone.)

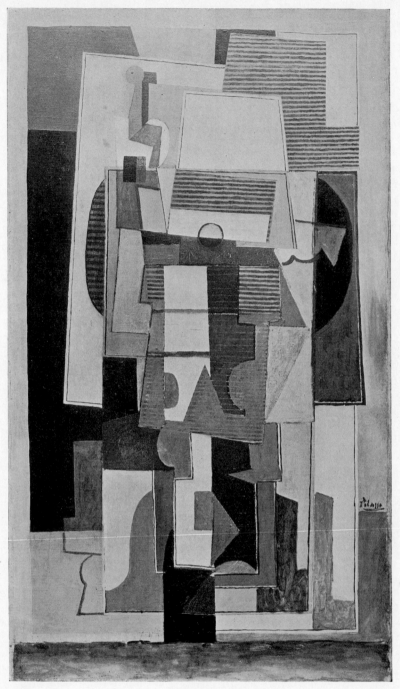

147

145. The Window. 1919 (dated). Gouache, 13¾ x 9¾ inches. Lent anonymously.

One of the most complete of a long series of similar compositions in which cubist technique is used superficially by comparison with the very abstract Table, opposite.

146. Table before a Window. 1919 (dated). Oil, 11⅛ x 9 inches. Lent anonymously.

147. The Table. 1919-20. Oil, 51 x 29⅝ inches. Lent by the Smith College Museum of Art, Northampton, Mass.

148. Still Life on a Table. 1920 (dated). Oil, 8¾ x 5 inches. Lent anonymously.

149. Landscape. 1920 (P). Oil, 20½ x 27½ inches. Lent by the artist.

Compare the early cubist landscape, no. 80, and the contemporary "classic" landscape, no. 156.

145

149

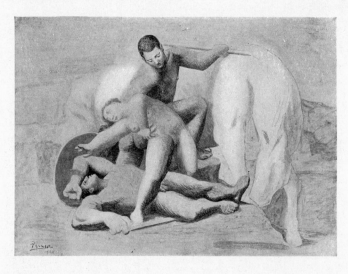

150

150. The Rape. 1920(dated). Tempera on wood, 9⅜ x 12⅞ inches. Lent by Philip L. Goodwin.

151. Centaur and Woman. September 12, 1920(dated). Ink, 7⅞ x 10½ inches. Lent by Gilbert Seldes. Inscribed: "12-9-20 Pour le ménage Seldes son ami Picasso." The American, Gilbert Seldes, later translated into English the Lysistrata of Aristophanes for which Picasso made illustrations (no. 270).

151

153

152. **Two Women by the Sea.** September 4, 1920(dated). Pencil, 29½ x 41¼ inches. Lent anonymously, courtesy the Worcester Art Museum.

153. **Four Classic Figures.** 1921(dated). Tempera on wood, 4 x 6 inches. Lent anonymously.

154. **Women by the Sea.** April 29, 1921(dated). Pencil, 9⅛ x 13 inches. Lent by Mrs. Charles J. Liebman.

154

155

155. Two Seated Women. 1920(dated). Oil, 76¾ x 64¼ inches. Lent by Walter P. Chrysler, Jr.
One of the most imposing of Picasso's compositions of colossal nudes.

156. Landscape. 1921 (dated). Pastel, 19½ x 25¼ inches. Lent by Walter P. Chrysler, Jr.

Picasso's "classic" period includes a number of styles ranging from the ponderous giantesses, opposite, to the attenuated diaphanous "néo-grec" figures of the Three Graces of 1924, no. 184. Both figure styles recall a similar contrast between the "colossal" and "attenuated" styles of the 16th century mannerists — and also Picasso's own work of 1905-06 (nos. 31, 67).

157. Hand.   January 20, 1921(dated). Pastel, 8¼ x 12⅝ inches. Lent by Walter P. Chrysler, Jr.

157

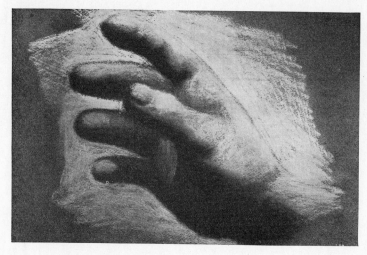

158

158. **Classic Head.** 1921. Pastel, 25¼ x 19¼ inches. Lent anonymously, courtesy the Worcester Art Museum. *The direct inspiration of Greco-Roman sculpture is here evident.*

159. **Bathing Woman.** 1921? Oil on wood, 5⅞ x 3⅞ inches. Lent by James Thrall Soby.

160. **The Wrestlers.** March 8, 1921. Lithograph, 4 x 7⅝ inches (G. 229). Collection The Museum of Modern Art, New York, gift of Mrs. Saidie A. May.

161. **Standing Nude.** 1921?(dated). Oil, 10⅝ x 8¾ inches. Lent by Mrs. Lloyd Bruce Wescott.

162. **Still Life.** January 8, 1921(dated). Gouache, 8¼ x 10¼ inches. Lent by Walter P. Chrysler, Jr.

163. **Girl in a Yellow Hat.** April 16, 1921(dated). Pastel, 41¼ x 29½ inches. Lent by Walter P. Chrysler, Jr. *This figure, while it retains the cubist use of transparent planes, looks forward in its flowing calligraphic curves to paintings of the late 1920's (nos. 210, 213).*

162

163

164

164. Three Musicians (Three Masks). Fontainebleau, summer 1921(dated). Oil, 80¾ x 88½ inches. Lent anonymously.

The climax of Picasso's synthetic cubism, at least in its rectilinear phase (1915-1922), is surely these two great compositions generally called the Three Musicians. *Their superb decorative beauty and, no less, their mysterious majesty, place them among Picasso's masterpieces.*

page 108

165

165. Three Musicians. Fontainebleau, summer 1921(dated). Oil, 80 x 74 inches. Lent by the Museum of Living Art, New York University.

The two versions of the Three Musicians are about the same height but this one is somewhat narrower, and more compact in composition. This is said to be the later version by a few weeks.

166

166. Guitar. 1922(dated). Oil, 32⅛ x 45⅞ inches. Lent by Paul Willert.

167. The Race. 1922. Tempera on wood, 12⅞ x 16¼ inches. Lent by the artist. Reproduced in color as frontispiece. This design was subsequently used for the curtain of the ballet Le Train Bleu produced in 1924 (see p. 192).

168. Nude. 1922? Pencil, 16¼ x 11¼ inches. Lent by Frank Crowninshield.

169. Standing Nude. 1922(dated). Oil on wood, 7½ x 5½ inches. Lent by the Wadsworth Atheneum.

170. Head of a Man. 1922? Pastel, 25⅝ x 19¾ inches. Lent by Mrs. Charles H. Russell, Jr.

169

170

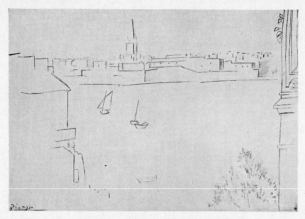

171

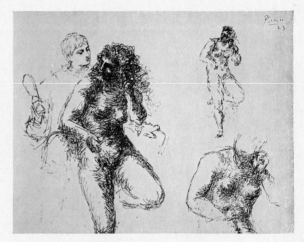

172

173

174

171. View of St. Malo (Dinard?)   1922. Ink and pencil, 11⅛ x 16⅛ inches. Lent anonymously.

172. Studies of Nude.   1923(dated). Ink, 9⅜ x 11½ inches. Lent anonymously.

173. The Pipes of Pan.   1923. Ink, 9¼ x 12⅛ inches. Lent by John Nicholas Brown.

174. The Sigh.   1923(dated). Oil and charcoal, 23¾ x 19¾ inches. Lent by James Thrall Soby.

175

175. Woman. 1922-23. Etching on zinc, 4½ x 3 inches; 2nd state (G. 99). Lent by the Weyhe Gallery. Made
for the first fifty-six copies of a book by Zervos, Picasso, Oeuvre, 1920-1926. Paris, Editions Cahiers d'Art,
1926. This copy is no. 40.

*About 1918 Picasso began to paint cubist pictures in which the curved line dominated the straight. "Curvi-
linear" cubism is well seen in this etching. Contrast the rectilinear* Violinist *of 1918, no. 140.*

176. The Three Bathers, III. 1922-23. Etching on zinc, 7 x 5⅛ inches (G. 108b). Lent by Mrs. John D. Rockefeller, Jr.

177. La Coiffure. 1923. Lithograph, 10¼ x 6½ inches (G. 234). Lent by Jean Goriany.

178. Head of a Young Man. 1923? Black crayon on pink paper, 23 x 17⅛ inches. Lent by the Brooklyn
Museum.

179

179. Woman in White.   1923. Oil, 39 x 31½ inches. The Museum of Modern Art, New York, Lillie P. Bliss
    Collection.

Picasso's ability to breathe new life and charm into a style so exhausted by overuse as the neo-classic is dem-
onstrated by the Woman in White.

180

180. By the Sea.   1923 (dated). Oil on wood, 32 x 39½ inches. Lent by Walter P. Chrysler, Jr.

This painting with its humorous and violent foreshortening is said to have been intended as a burlesque of the long tradition of solemn "bather" compositions by Cézanne, Matisse, Friesz and others, of which a typical example is Matisse's Women by the Sea *formerly in the Folkwang Museum, Essen (illustrated* Henri-Matisse, *Museum of Modern Art, 1931, pl. 17). Picasso himself is, however, one of the most prolific masters of the "bather" tradition.*

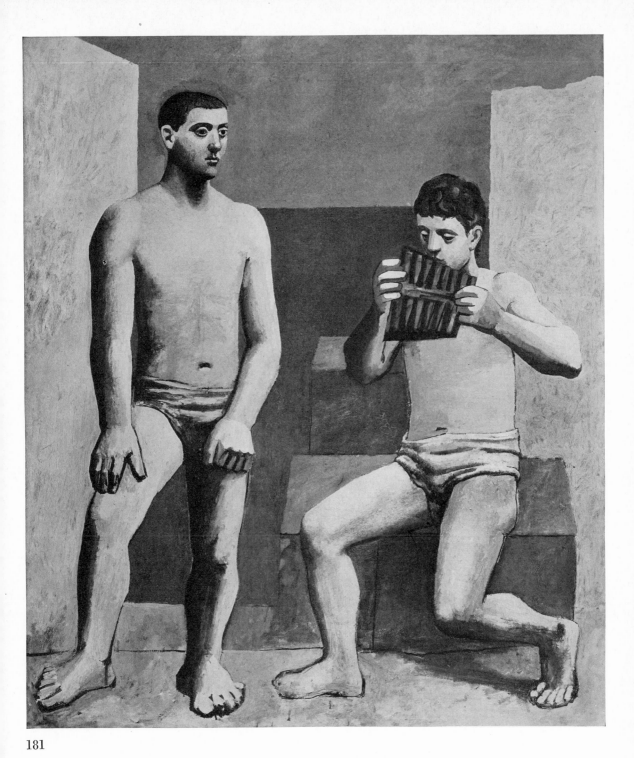

181

181. The Pipes of Pan (La Flûte de Pan). 1923. Oil, 80½ x 68⅝ inches. Lent by the artist.

This and the Two Seated Women, *no. 155, are generally considered the capital works of Picasso's classic period.*

182

182. Musical Instruments. 1923 (dated). Oil, 38 x 51 inches. Lent by Mrs. Patrick C. Hill.

One of a small group of curvilinear cubist still lifes of very sombre color. Compare with the brilliant rectilinear cubist still life of the previous year, no. 166.

183. Still Life. 1924. Conté crayon with oil wash, 9¼ x 6¾ inches. Lent by the Museum of Living Art, New York University.

184. Three Graces. 1924. Oil and charcoal, 78⅞ x 59 inches. Lent by the artist.

Picasso's "classic" period began with the Ingres-like drawings of 1915-20, continued with the figures more directly inspired by Greco-Roman art, some of them of colossal proportions (1920-23), and came to an end, so far as paintings are concerned, with the refined and colorless elegance of the Three Graces.

84

185. Still Life with a Mandolin and Biscuit.   May 16, 1924(dated on back). Oil, 38¼ x 51¼ inches. Lent anonymously.

One of the earliest in the series of large brilliantly colored still life compositions which continues into 1926. Related in its soft curves to the dark compositions of the previous year (no. 182).

186.   Still Life with Biscuits.   1924(dated). Oil and sand, 32 x 39¾ inches. Lent anonymously.

185

187

187. The Red Tablecloth (Le Tapis Rouge).   December 1924 (dated). Oil, $38\frac{3}{4}$ x $51\frac{3}{8}$ inches. Lent anonymously.

The most famous of the series of large interiors and still life compositions painted during the years 1924-26.

188

188. Woman with a Mandolin (La Musicienne). 1925(dated). Oil, 51⅜ x 38⅝ inches. Lent anonymously.

189

189. The Fish Net. Juan les Pins, summer 1925 (dated). Oil, $39\frac{3}{4}$ x $32\frac{3}{8}$ inches. Lent anonymously.

190

191

190. The Three Dancers. 1925. Oil, 84⅝ x 56¼ inches. Lent by the artist.

The Three Dancers, *painted only a year later than the* Three Graces, *no. 184, comes as a sudden and surprising interruption to the series of monumental still life compositions and flat linear figures like the* Woman with a Mandolin, *no. 188. Instead of static, mildly cubist decoration, the* Three Dancers *confronts us with a vision striking in its physical and emotional violence. Seen objectively as representations of nature, cubist paintings such as the* Three Musicians *of 1921 are grotesque enough (nos. 164, 165) — but their distortions are comparatively objective and formal whereas the frightful, grinning mask and convulsive action of the left-hand figure of the* Three Dancers *cannot be resolved into an exercise in esthetic relationships, magnificent as the canvas is from a purely formal point of view. The* Three Dancers *is in fact a turning point in Picasso's art almost as radical as was the* Demoiselles d'Avignon *(no. 71). The left-hand dancer especially foreshadows new periods of his art in which psychologically disturbing energies reinforce or, depending on one's point of view, adulterate his ever changing achievements in the realm of form.*

191. The Ram's Head. Juan les Pins, summer 1925 (dated). Oil, 32⅛ x 39½ inches. Lent anonymously.

The sumptuous still life series was continued after the Three Dancers *until 1926. Among the richest and most compactly ordered are the somewhat sinister* Ram's Head, *above, and* The Studio, *on the following page.*

192

192. The Studio. Juan les Pins, summer 1925. Oil, 38⅝ x 51⅝ inches. Private collection.

193. Still Life with a Bottle of Wine. 1926(dated). Oil, 38⅝ x 51¼ inches. Lent anonymously.

193

195

194

199

194. **Three Dancers Resting.** 1925(dated). Ink, 13¾ x 9⅞ inches. Lent anonymously.

195. **Four Ballet Dancers.** 1925(dated). Ink, 13½ x 10 inches. Collection the Museum of Modern Art, New York, gift of Mrs. John D. Rockefeller, Jr.

196. **Two Ballet Dancers Resting.** 1925(dated). Ink, 13⅝ x 9⅞ inches. Lent by the Wadsworth Atheneum.

197. **Pas de deux (Two Ballet Dancers).** 1925. Ink, 24½ x 18⅞ inches. Lent by Mrs. Ray Slater Murphy.

198. **Head of a Woman.** 1925. Lithograph, 5 x 4⅝ inches (G. 240). Lent by the Buchholz Gallery.

199. **Head.** 1926. Charcoal and white chalk, 25 x 19 inches. Lent by Walter P. Chrysler, Jr.

Picasso's "classic" figure drawings of 1923 to 1925 are more spontaneous than the comparatively calculated studies of the "Ingres" period, 1917-20.

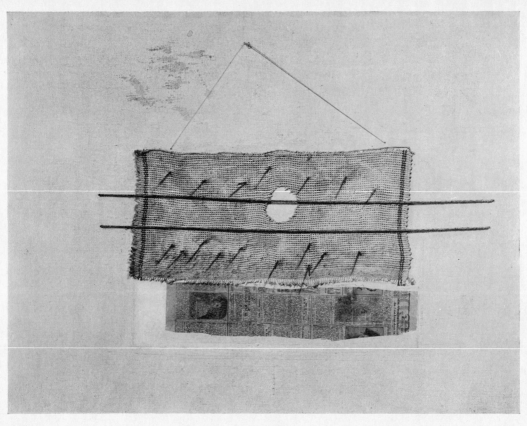

200

200. **Guitar.** 1926(P). Canvas with string, pasted paper, oil paint, and cloth fixed with two inch nails, points out; 38¼ x 51¼ inches. Lent by the artist.

201. **Guitar.** 1926(P). Panel with string, bamboo and cloth applied with tacks; 51⅛ x 38¼ inches. Lent by the artist.

These two compositions recall the radical experimentation with a variety of unconventional materials in the cubist collages and relief constructions of 1913-14 (no. 115). The year 1926 was in several ways a time of renewed experiment.

202. **Interior.** 1926. Lithograph, 8½ x 10¾ inches (G. 241). Lent by Mrs. John D. Rockefeller, Jr.

203. **Reading.** 1926. Lithograph, 12⅛ x 9⅛ inches (G. 242). Lent by Mrs. John D. Rockefeller, Jr.

204. **The Painter and His Model.** 1926(dated). Ink, 11¼ x 14¾ inches. Lent anonymously. Study for the illustrations of Balzac's Le Chef-d'Oeuvre Inconnu.

205. **Painter with a Model Knitting.** 1927. Etching, 7⅝ x 11⅜ inches (G. 126). Illustration for Balzac, Le Chef-d'Oeuvre Inconnu. Paris, Vollard, 1931. Illustrated with 13 etchings and 121 wood engravings, after drawings, by Picasso (G. 123-35). Lent by Mrs. Lloyd Bruce Wescott. The abstract character of the painting described in Balzac's story and shown in the etching is noteworthy.

205a. **Wood engravings after ink drawings of 1926.** Illustrations for Balzac, Le Chef-d'Oeuvre Inconnu. (See no. 205.) Picasso filled a sketch book with scores of similar designs of dots and connecting lines, some apparently abstract, others representing violins, guitars, tables and figures.

206. **The Nude Model.** 1927. Etching, 11 x 7⅝ inches; 2nd state (G. 119, II). Collection the Art Institute of Chicago.

205

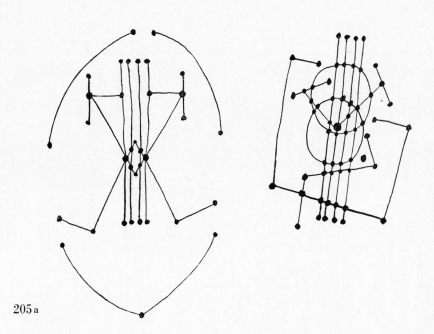

205 a

207

208

207. Seated Woman. 1926-27(dated on back). Oil, 51½ x 38½ inches. Collection the Museum of Modern Art, New York.

208. Woman in an Armchair. January 1927(dated on back). Oil, 51⅜ x 38¼ inches. Lent by the artist.

Early in 1927 Picasso was developing the manner first announced by the left hand figure of the Three Dancers, *of 1925 (no. 190).*

209

209. Seated Woman. 1927(dated). Oil on wood, 51⅛ x 38¼ inches. Lent by James Thrall Soby.

The complex arabesque of curves of the Seated Woman (no. 207) is simplified in this version of the same subject — one of the most awe-inspiring of Picasso's figures.

210

210. Figure. 1927. Oil on plywood, 51⅛ x 38⅛ inches. Lent by the artist.

In 1927 Picasso began to paint figures and heads in which the anatomy is distorted and dislocated with an extravagance exceeding even that of the Woman in an Armchair *(no. 208). In the* Figure *reproduced above the human form has undergone a metamorphosis so radical that foot, head, breast and arm are not readily recognizable. Only a few rather isolated cubist works of 1913-14 anticipate such fantastic anatomy, notably the* Head, *no. 117, and a series of drawings (compare bibl. 97, pl. 5-8). But the design of the* Figure *in its severity and firmness also recalls the finest cubist* papiers collés *(nos. 107, 117).*

211. Seated Woman. 1927. Oil, 8½ x 4¾ inches. Lent by Sidney Janis.

212

212. **The Studio.** 1927-28 (dated on back). Oil, 59 x 91 inches. Collection the Museum of Modern Art, New York, gift of Walter P. Chrysler, Jr.

The sparse severity of the preceding painting is seen again in this large, precisely calculated composition of straight lines and rectangles recalling once more the cubism of 1912-13 (nos. 104, 107). At the left is the painter, brush in hand; at the right a table covered by a red cloth on which rests a bowl of fruit and a white plaster bust, a subject somewhat comparable to the The Studio, no. 192.

213. **Painting (Running Minotaur).** April 1928 (dated on back). Oil, 63¾ x 51¼ inches. Lent by the artist.

Compare in style with the Figure, no. 210. A pasted paper of a similar subject was used as a cartoon for a large Gobelin tapestry executed in 1936 and listed following no. 360.

213

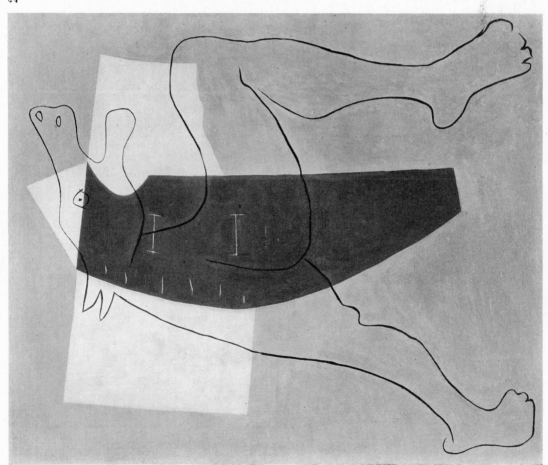

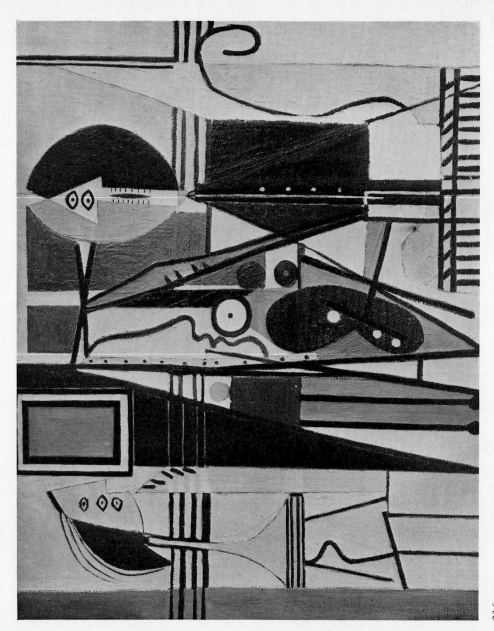

214. Head. 1928? Construction in painted metal. Not in exhibition.

In 1928 Picasso began to work again in three dimensions, in painted metal constructions such as this, in iron wire no. 219, and in plaster. This Head is related to the heads in the Painter and his Model, above.

215. The Studio. 1928. Oil, 63⅝ x 51⅛ inches. Lent by the artist.

216. The Painter and His Model. 1928 (dated). Oil, 51⅝ x 63⅞ inches. Lent by Sidney Janis.

Similar in subject to the somewhat earlier Studio, no. 212, but more elaborate and concentrated. A detailed analysis of this painting by Harriet Janis is given in bibl. 20, p. 101. Briefly: the painter sits at the right, brush or palette knife in his right hand, palette in his left. At the left is the model. Between them is the canvas on which the artist has drawn a profile which is conventionally realistic in contrast to the heads of the painter and model. By doing this Picasso, with a certain humor, reverses the normal relationship of art and "nature" such as is shown in the etching, no. 205. The projection of the image in the artist's brain upon the canvas is symbolized by lines which issue from the head of the artist, cross at the tip of the palette knife or brush, and strike the canvas at the top of the painted profile.

214

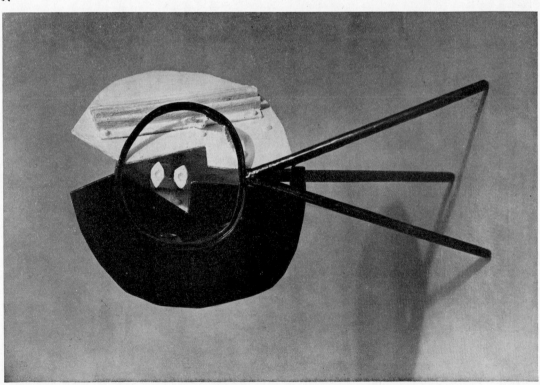

218

217

217. Head of a woman. 1927 or 1928. Oil and sand, 21⅝ x 21⅝ inches. Lent by the artist.

Teeth, eyes, hair, nose and breasts are here redistributed with an easy virtuosity comparable to that shown in the Figure, no. 210.

218. Head. 1928. Oil, 21¾ x 13 inches. Lent anonymously.
Compare with the Head of 1914, no. 117.

220

219. **Construction.** 1928? Iron wire. Not in exhibition. *Compare with the paintings, nos. 212 and 216.*

220. **On the Beach.** Dinard, 1928. Oil, 7½ x 12¾ inches. Lent by George L. K. Morris.

This and the following painting belong to a famous series of small beach scenes done at Dinard in the summer of 1928. Compare with the figures in the Three Dancers, no. 190.

221. **Beach Scene.** Dinard, August 21, 1928 (dated). Oil, 6½ x 9⅞ inches. Lent by Rosenberg and Helft Ltd.

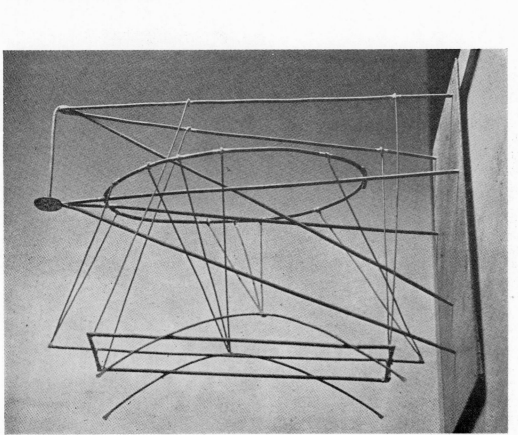

219

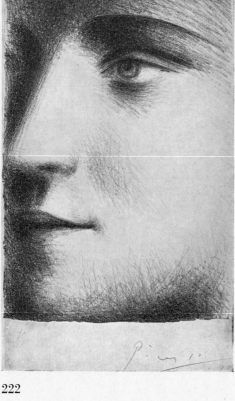

222

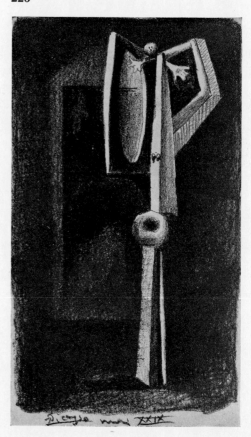

223

222. Face. 1928. Lithograph, 8 x 5½ inches (G. 243). Lent by Mrs. John D. Rockefeller, Jr.

After 1915 Picasso at no time has devoted himself to cubist, "abstract" or "surrealist" work to the exclusion of more "realistic" styles.

223. Figure. May 1929. Transfer lithograph, 9 x 5¼ inches (G. 246). Published for subscribers of the review Le Manuscrit Autographe. Paris, A. Blaizot et fils. Plate hors-texte of no. 21, May-June 1929. Lent by Jean Goriany.

One of many sculpturesque figures developed from the flat two-dimensional style of the Figure, no. 210. Compare with the cubist perspective drawings of 1913-14, no. 114.

224. Bather. 1929(dated). Oil, 16¼ x 10¾ inches. Lent by Pierre Loeb.

225. Two Nudes. September 30, 1930. Etching, 12 5/16 x 8 13/16 inches (G. 199b). Lent by Mrs. John D. Rockefeller, Jr.

226.

226. **Combat of Perseus and Phineus over Andromeda.** 1930. Etching, 8¾ x 6⅝ inches (G. 152). Illustration for Ovid, Les Métamorphoses. Lausanne, Skira, 1931. Illustrated with 30 etchings by Picasso (G. 143-72). Lent by the Marie Harriman Gallery.

227. **Death of Orpheus.** September 16, 1930. Etching, 9 x 6⅝ inches; unpublished plate for Ovid, Les Métamorphoses, book XI; 1st state without the remarque (G. 174, I). Lent by Monroe Wheeler.

228

228. Woman in an Armchair (Métamorphose). 1929(dated). Oil, 36⅜ x 28¾ inches. Lent anonymously.

229. Woman in an Armchair. May 5, 1929(dated on back). Oil, 76¾ x 51⅛ inches. Lent by the artist.

Two paintings of similar subjects done in the same year. Compare the figure opposite with the Woman in an Armchair, *no. 208, of 1927, and the left-hand figure of the* Three Dancers, *no. 190, of 1925.*

229

230

230. Bather, Standing.   May 26, 1929 (dated on back). Oil, 76¾ x 51⅛ inches. Lent by the artist.

Compare with the Woman in an Armchair, *no. 228.*

231

231. Seated Bather. 1929. Oil, 63⅞ x 51⅛ inches. Lent by Mrs. Meric Callery.

One of the most important paintings of the so-called "bone" period. Compare nos. 233, 234.

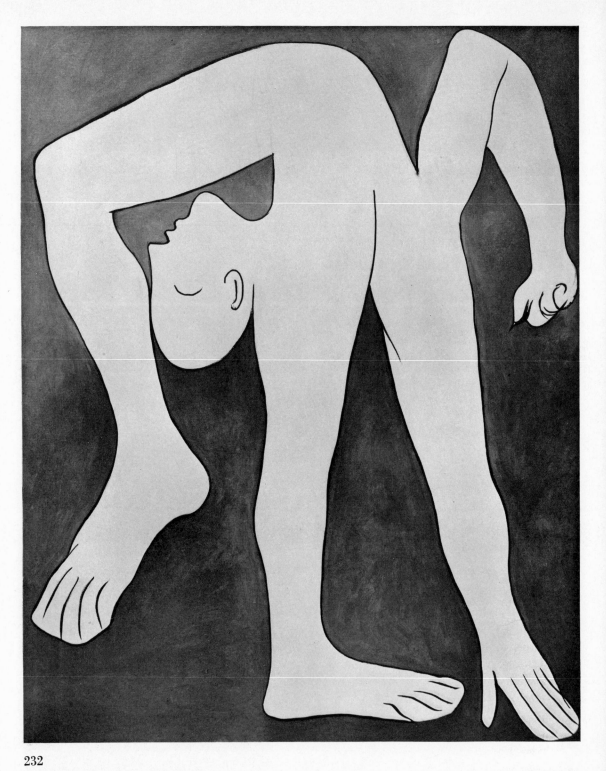

232

232. Acrobat. January 18, 1930 (dated on back). Oil, 63⅞ x 51⅜ inches. Lent by the artist.
Compare the Swimming Woman *of November 1929, no. 235.*

233

233. Crucifixion. February 7, 1930(dated on back). Oil on wood, 20 x 26 inches. Lent by the artist.

Probably Picasso's first painting of a biblical subject since 1904 (compare also no. 13). For studies for this picture see bibl. 40, plates 124 ff. See also the related studies for a crucifixion "after Grünewald" done in September-October 1932 (bibl. 34, pp. 30-32).

234. Project for a Monument (Métamorphose). February 19, 1930(dated). Oil on wood, 26 x 19⅛ inches. Lent by Walter P. Chrysler, Jr.

Kahnweiler says that Picasso had in mind at this time colossal monuments in reinforced concrete to be built on mountains overlooking the Riviera.

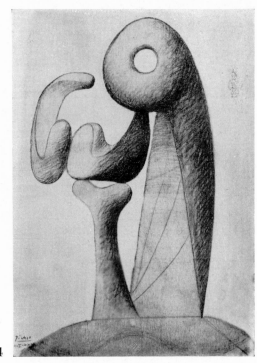

234

235. Swimming Woman. November 1929 (dated on back). Oil, 63⅞ x 51⅛ inches. Lent by the artist.

Should come chronologically before the Acrobat, no. 232, which it resembles.

236. By the Sea. Juan les Pins, August 22, 1930 (dated on back). Plaster and sand relief, 10⅝ x 13¾ inches. Lent by the artist.

Unfortunately the war has prevented the inclusion in the exhibition of other examples of Picasso's sculpture of the past fifteen years. This is a comparatively minor example.

236

235

237

237. Figure Throwing a Stone. March 8, 1931 (dated on back). Oil, 51¼ x 76⅝ inches. Lent by the artist.

238

238. **Pitcher and Bowl of Fruit.** February 22, 1931(dated). Oil, 51½ x 64 inches. Lent by Rosenberg and Helft Ltd.

In 1931 Picasso painted a series of large still lifes and interiors using a kind of curvilinear cubist method of composition. This, one of the finest, recalls medieval stained glass in color.

239. **Two Nudes in a Tree.** July 4, 1931. Etching, 14⅞ x 11¾ inches (G. 204). Lent by the Weyhe Gallery. Geiser mentions 3 proofs only but this is numbered 7.

240. **Still Life on a Table.** March 11, 1931(dated on back). Oil, 76¾ x 51⅛ inches. Lent by the artist.

When this large, brilliantly colored, and generally flamboyant painting was pulled out from a stack of canvases during the selection of the exhibition, Picasso remarked with a smile, emphasizing the word "morte": "En voilà une nature morte."

241. **Reclining Woman.** November 9, 1931(dated on back). Oil, 76¾ x 51¼ inches. Lent by the artist.

242. **Seated Nude.** December 21, 1931(dated on back). Oil, 63⅞ x 51⅛ inches. Lent by the artist.

240

244

page 154

245

243. **Still Life with Tulips.** March 2, 1932 (dated on back). Oil, 51¼ x 38¼ inches. Lent by A. Bellanger.

244. **Nude on a Black Couch.** March 9, 1932 (dated). Oil, 63¾ x 51¼ inches. Lent by Mrs. Meric Callery.

245. **The Mirror.** Paris, March 12, 1932 (dated on back). Oil, 51¼ x 38¼ inches. Lent by the artist.

In the spring of 1932 Picasso produced with amazing energy a long series of large canvases of women, usually sleeping or seated, unlike anything he had done before in their bold color and great sweeping curves.

246

246. Girl Before a Mirror. Paris, March 14, 1932 (dated on back). Oil, 63¾ x 51¼ inches. Collection the Museum of Modern Art, New York, gift of Mrs. Simon Guggenheim.

The brilliant color, heavy lines, complex design and lozenge-shaped background suggest Gothic stained glass. In the summer of 1932, at the time of the great retrospective exhibition of his work, Picasso said he preferred this painting to any of the others in the long series he had completed that spring.

page 156

247

247. Figure in a Red Chair.   1932. Oil, 51⅛ x 38¼ inches. Lent by the artist.

248. Seated Woman and Bearded Head.   1932. Ink and pencil, 11⅛ x 10⅛ inches. Lent by Walter P. Chrysler, Jr.

The left-hand figure is a study for the painting, Figure in a Red Chair, *no. 247. An interesting contrast between two figures drawn on the same paper but in very different styles.*

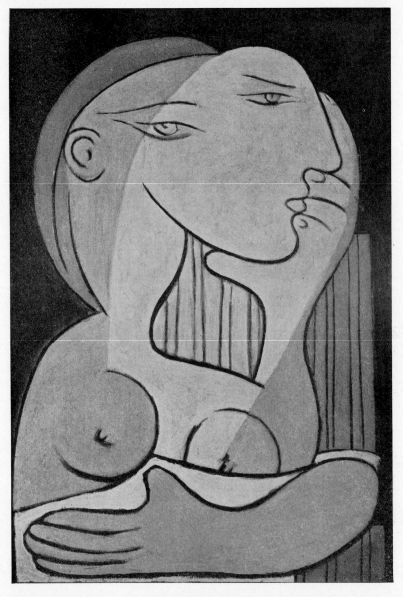

249

249. Seated Woman. 1932. Oil on wood, 29¼ x 20⅝ inches. Lent by Lee A. Ault.

250. Woman Sleeping. 1932. Oil, 39⅜ x 32 inches. Lent by J. Thannhauser.

251. Figures. 1932? Etching, 4¹⁵⁄₁₆ x 3⅝ inches. Lent by the Weyhe Gallery. One of a set of six plates by various artists published by S. W. Hayter in 1937 and sold for Spanish relief. The design is in the style of certain drawings done toward the end of 1932 (bibl. 138, pl. 5, 6), but the etching may have been executed in 1936-37.

252. Bathers and Diver. 1932? Etching printed in black ink on collage of colored papers, 5½ x 4⁷⁄₁₆ inches. Lent by the Weyhe Gallery. Design is very similar in style to the painting, no. 254, of December 1932.

253. Bathers and Diver. 1932? Etching printed in white ink on collage of colored papers, 5½ x 4⁷⁄₁₆ inches. Lent by the Weyhe Gallery. Same plate as no. 252.

254. Three Women by the Sea. November 28, 1932 (dated on back). Oil, 32 x 39⅜ inches. Lent by the artist. Compare with the Women by the Sea of 1923, no. 180.

255. Two Women on the Beach. Paris, January 11, 1933 (dated on back). Oil, 28⅞ x 36¼ inches. Lent by the artist.

254

255

256

256. Plaster Head and Bowl of Fruit.   January 29, 1933(dated). Oil, 28⅞ x 36¼ inches. Lent by Mr. and
   Mrs. Joseph Pulitzer, Jr.

257. Silenus.   Cannes, July 14, 1933(dated). Gouache, 15½ x 19¾ inches. Lent by A. Conger Goodyear.

258. Two Figures on the Beach.   Cannes, July 28, 1933(dated). Ink, 15¾ x 19⅝ inches. Lent anonymously.

259. Sculpture in Picasso's studio at Gisors, 1933.   Photograph by A. E. Gallatin.

*Most of Picasso's recent sculpture has been done at his country estate, Boisgeloup, near Gisors on the
border of Normandy. In Mr. Gallatin's photograph are two of a series of the large plaster heads, one of
which appears in the painting illustrated above. (For further illustrations of his sculpture see bibl. 34
and 39.)*

259

260

261

260. Sculptor and His Statue. Cannes, July 20, 1933 (dated). Gouache, 15⅜ x 19½ inches. Lent anonymously.

261. On the Beach. Cannes, July 11, 1933 (dated). Watercolor and ink, 15⅝ x 19¾ inches. Lent by Dr. and Mrs. Allan Roos. One of the most surrealist of Picasso's long series of 1933 gouaches and drawings (nos. 257, 258, 260, 261).

262. Circus (Acrobats). Paris, February 6, 1933 (dated on back). Oil, 18⅛ x 14⅞ inches. Lent by the artist.

263. Bull Fight. Boisgeloup, July 27, 1934 (dated). Oil, 19¾ x 25¾ inches. Lent by the Phillips Memorial Gallery, Washington.

The Bull Fight as a subject for painting had interested Picasso briefly in 1900 and again shortly after the war of 1914-18, but during the past few years he has used it again and again apparently for its symbolic significance as well as for its pictorial interest. (See nos. 10, 273, 274, and the Guernica mural with its numerous studies, no. 280 and following.)

262

263

264

265

264.   Girl Writing.   1934. Oil. Lent by Peter Watson.
For a remarkable analysis of this canvas see Melville, bibl. 138.

265.   Two Girls Reading.   March 28, 1934 (dated on back). Oil, 31⅞ x 25½ inches. Lent by Mrs. John W. Garrett.

268

269

266. Interior with Figures. 1934. Oil, about 9 x 12 inches. Lent by Mme. Christian Zervos.

267. Bull Fight. Boisgeloup, September 9, 1934 (dated). Oil, 13 x 16⅛ inches. Lent by Henry P. McIlhenny. Illustrated: Fantastic Art, Dada, Surrealism, The Museum of Modern Art, 1936, pl. 260.

268. Interior with a Girl Drawing. Paris, February 12, 1935 (dated on back). Oil, 51⅛ x 76⅝ inches. Lent by Mrs. Meric Callery. *A series of studies for this composition are illustrated in bibl. 39, following p. 244.*

269. Sleeping Girl. February 3, 1935 (dated on back). Oil, 18⅛ x 21⅝ inches. Lent by Walter P. Chrysler, Jr.

270

273

270. **Myrrhina and Kinesias.** 1934. Etching, 8⅝ x 6 inches. Illustration for Aristophanes, Lysistrata, a new version by Gilbert Seldes. New York, Limited Editions Club, 1934. Illustrated with 6 etchings and 33 drawings by Picasso. Lent by George Macy.

271. **Study for Lysistrata illustrations.** Paris, January 4, 1934(dated). Ink and wash, 9½ x 13¼ inches. Lent by the Museum of Living Art, New York University.

272. **Copper plate for Lysistrata illustration** (see no. 270). 1934. 8½ x 5¾ inches. Collection the Museum of Modern Art, New York, gift of J. B. Neumann.

273. **Minotauromachy.** 1935. Etching, 19½ x 27¼ inches. Lent by Henry P. McIlhenny.

Probably Picasso's most important print.

274. **Dreams and Lies of Franco** (Sueño y Mentira de Franco). January 8, 1937. Etching and aquatint, 12¼ x 16⅜ inches; 2nd state. Lent by J. B. Neumann. Plate contains nine designs.

275. **Dreams and Lies of Franco** (Sueño y Mentira de Franco). January 9-June 7, 1937. Etching and aquatint, 12⅜ x 16⅝ inches; 2nd state. Lent by J. B. Neumann. Plate contains nine designs, four of which, nos. 4, 7, 8, 9, were etched on June 7th during the painting of the Guernica mural, no. 280. See illustration on page 171.

These two plates were published together with a facsimile of a prose poem by Picasso, part of which is reproduced on the following page together with an English translation of the whole. The eighteen designs were subsequently printed separately in postcard format and sold for the benefit of the Spanish Republican Government.

fandango de lechuzas escabeche de espadas de pulpos de mal agüero estropajo de pelos de coronillas de pie en medio de la sartén en pelotas — puesto sobre el cucurucho del sorbete de bacalao frito en la sarna de su corazón — la boca llena de la jalea de chinches de sus palabras — cuya bolsa del plato de caracoles trenzando tripas — meñique en erección ni breva — con. Edig. del arte de mal tejer y teñir nubes — la basura

— P. Picasso

DREAMS AND LIES OF FRANCO

fandango of shivering owls souse of swords of evil-omened polyps scouring brush of hairs from priests' tonsures standing naked in the middle of the frying-pan — placed upon the ice cream cone of codfish fried in the scabs of his lead-ox heart — his mouth full of the chinch-bug jelly of his words — sleigh-bells of the plate of snails braiding guts — little finger in erection neither grape nor fig — commedia dell'arte of poor weaving and dyeing of clouds — beauty creams from the garbage wagon — rape of maids in tears and in snivels — on his shoulder the shroud stuffed with sausages and mouths — rage distorting the outline of the shadow which flogs his teeth driven in the sand and the horse open wide to the sun which reads it to the flies that stitch to the knots of the net full of anchovies the sky-rocket of lilies — torch of lice where the dog is knot of rats and hiding-place of the palace of old rags — the banners which fry in the pan writhe in the black of the ink-sauce shed in the drops of blood which shoot him — the street rises to the clouds tied by its

feet to the sea of wax which rots its entrails and the veil which covers it sings and dances wild with pain — the flight of fishing rods and the alhigui alhigui of the first-class burial of the moving van — the broken wings rolling upon the spider's web of dry bread and clear water of the paella of sugar and velvet which the lash paints upon his cheeks — the light covers its eyes before the mirror which apes it and the nougat bar of the flames bites its lips at the wound — cries of children cries of women cries of birds cries of flowers cries of timbers and of stones cries of bricks cries of furniture of beds of chairs of curtains of pots of cats and of papers cries of odors which claw at one another cries of smoke pricking the shoulder of the cries which stew in the cauldron and of the rain of birds which inundates the sea which gnaws the bone and breaks its teeth biting the cotton wool which the sun mops up from the plate which the purse and the pocket hide in the print which the foot leaves in the rock.

278

276. Pitcher and Candle. Paris, January 30, 1937 (dated). Oil, 15 x 18⅛ inches. Lent by Rosenberg and Helft Ltd.

In 1937 and 1938 Picasso produced a series of decorative, richly painted still life compositions (nos. 276, 277, 278, 341, 358). Their gay objectivity is in marked contrast to the agonies of the Guernica mural and disquieting surrealist atmosphere of the Girls with a Toy Boat, no. 279, and the Girl with a Cock, no. 345.

277. Still Life. January 21, 1937 (dated). Oil, 19½ x 24 inches. Lent by the Bignou Gallery.

278. Negro Sculpture before a Window. April 19, 1937 (dated). Oil, 27¾ x 23⅝ inches. Lent anonymously.

279. Girls with a Toy Boat. February 12, 1937 (dated on back). Oil and charcoal, 51⅛ x 76¾ inches. Lent by Mrs. Meric Callery.

276

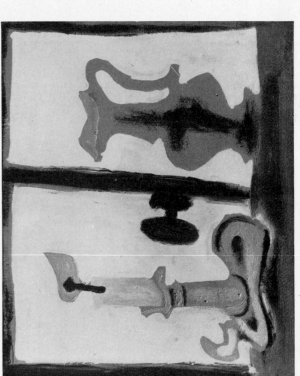

279

280

280. Guernica. May—early July? 1937. Oil on canvas, 11 feet 6 inches x 25 feet 8 inches. Lent by the artist.

On April 28, 1937 the Basque town of Guernica was reported destroyed by German bombing planes flying for General Franco. Picasso who had already taken the Loyalist side in his Dreams and Lies of Franco (nos. 274-75), immediately prepared to take an artist's revenge. Commissioned to paint a mural for the Spanish Government Building at the Paris World's Fair he began work on May 1st, just two days after the news of the catastrophe.

Picasso has given no exact explanation of Guernica. Briefly, one sees: at the right two women, one with arms raised before a burning house, the other rushing in toward the center of the picture; at the left a mother with a dead child, and on the ground the fragments of a warrior, one hand clutching a broken sword. At the center of the canvas is a dying horse pierced by a spear hurled from above; at the left a bull stands triumphantly surveying the scene.

Above, to the right of the center a figure leans from a window holding a lamp which throws an ineluctable light upon the carnage. And over all shines the radiant eye of day with the electric bulb of night for a pupil.

Guernica is painted entirely in black, white, and grey.

Although the Guernica is in no sense dependent on earlier works of Picasso, it is interesting to compare it with the Dreams and Lies of Franco (excepting the last four pictures which were done after Guernica) (nos. 274-75); the bull fights of 1934 (nos. 263, 267); the Crucifixion of 1930 (no. 233); and above all the Minotauromachy of 1935 (no. 273) in which several of the Guernica motifs appear but as symbols perhaps of personal, rather than of public, experience.

Fifty-nine studies for the Guernica (and a few "postscripts") are listed in the following pages. Many of these have interest as independent works of art; cumulatively they make it possible to study how Picasso has proceeded in composing one of the most important paintings of recent years.

Illustrated at the left is the first composition study, dated May 1st (no. 281). It is a shorthand notation showing the bull (left), the horse lying on its back (center) and the house with the figure in the window holding a lamp (right), all three of which were to appear in somewhat different form in the mural.

Below, dated May 9th, is the final pencil study for the whole composition which may be compared, detail for detail, with the final version, no. 280.

By May 11th, Picasso had outlined the full scale composition drawn on the 26 foot canvas, but in so doing had already revised the sketch of May 9th; and many other radical revisions were made on the canvas itself before it was completed.

Photographs of the mural in eight progressive stages and many of the studies are reproduced in Cahiers d'Art (see bibl. 39a).

281

294

281-340. Studies for Guernica, cataloged on the following pages.

288

281-340. *STUDIES FOR GUERNICA. Some of the later items were done after the completion of the mural and are therefore in the nature of postscripts.*

May 1

281-84. Composition studies. Pencil on blue paper, 8¼ x 10⅝ inches.

285. Study for the horse. Pencil on blue paper, 8¼ x 10½ inches.

286. Composition study. Pencil on gesso, 21⅛ x 25½ inches.

May 2

285. Study for the horse. Pencil on blue paper, 8¼ 28¾ inches.

288. Horse's head. Oil on canvas, 25½ x 36¼ inches.

289-90. Studies for horse's head. Pencil on blue paper, 8¼ x 6 inches, and 10½ x 8¼ inches.

Early May

291. Horse and Bull. Pencil on tan paper, 8⅞ x 4¾ inches.

May 8

292. Composition study. Pencil on white paper, 9½ x 17⅞ inches.

293. Horse and woman with dead child. Pencil on white paper, 9½ x 17⅞ inches.

May 9

294. Composition study. Pencil on white paper, 9½ x 17⅞ inches.

295. Woman with dead child on ladder. Pencil on white paper, 17⅞ x 9½ inches.

296. Woman with dead child. Ink on white paper, 9½ x 17⅞ inches.

May 10

297-98. Studies for the horse. Pencil on white paper, 9½ x 17⅞ inches.

299. Horse. Pencil and color crayon on white paper, 9½ x 17⅞ inches.

300. Bull's head. Pencil on white paper, 17⅞ x 9½ inches.

301. Woman with dead child. Color crayon and pencil on white paper, 9½ x 17⅞ inches.

May 11

302. Bull. Pencil on white paper, 9½ x 17⅞ inches.

May 13

303. Woman with dead child. Color crayon and pencil on white paper, 9½ x 17⅞ inches.

304. Head. Pencil and color crayon on white paper, 17⅞ x 9½ inches.

305. Hand with broken sword. Pencil on white paper, 9½ x 17⅞ inches.

May 20

306. Horse's head. Pencil on gray paper, 9½ x 11½ inches.

307. Horse's head. Pencil on white paper, 9¼ x 11½ inches.

308-09. Studies for bull's head. Pencil on gray tinted paper, 9¼ x 11½ inches.

293

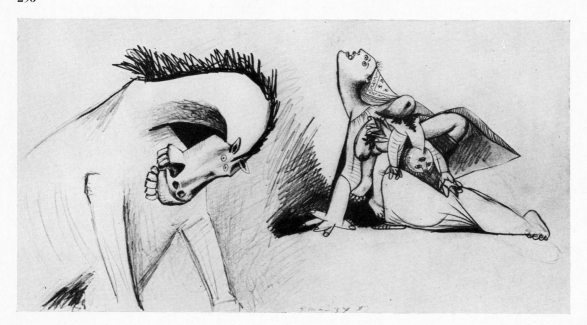

291

310. Head. Pencil and gouache on white paper, 11½ x 9¼ inches.

May 24

311-13. Heads. Pencil and gouache on white paper, 11½ x 9¼ inches.

May 27

314. Head. Pencil on gray paper, 9¼ x 11½ inches.

315. Man. Pencil and gouache on white paper, 9¼ x 11½ inches.

May 28

316. Woman with dead child. Pencil, ink and gouache on gray paper, 9¼ x 11½ inches.

317. Woman with dead child. Pencil, color crayon and oil on white paper, 9¼ x 11½ inches.

318. Weeping head. Pencil, color crayon and gouache on white paper, 9¼ x 11½ inches.

May 31

319. Head. Pencil, color crayon and gouache on white paper, 9¼ x 11½ inches.

June 3

320-22. Weeping heads. Pencil and color crayon on white paper, 9¼ x 11½ inches.

323. Head and horse's hoofs. Pencil and gouache on white paper, 9¼ x 11½ inches.

June 4

324-25. Heads. Pencil and gouache on white paper, 9¼ x 11½ inches.

June 8

326-27. Heads. Pencil and color crayon on white paper, 11½ x 9¼ inches.

June 13

328. Head. Pencil and color crayon on white paper, 11½ x 9¼ inches.

June 15

329. Weeping Head. Pencil and oil on canvas, 21⅝ x 18⅛ inches.

June 21

330. Weeping head. Oil on canvas, 21⅝ x 18⅛ inches.

June 22

331. Woman. Pencil and oil on canvas, 21⅝ x 18⅛ inches.

332. Weeping head. Pencil and gouache on cardboard, 4⅝ x 3½ inches.

July 2

333. Weeping Woman. Etching and aquatint, 27¼ x 19½ inches. First state, no. 6/15.

334. Weeping Woman. Etching and aquatint, 27¼ x 19½ inches. Second state, no. 4/15.

July 4

335. Weeping head. Ink on white paper, 10 x 6¾ inches.

July 6

336. Weeping head. Ink on tan paper, 6 x 4½ inches.

September 26

337. Composition study.   Oil on canvas, 76¾ x 51¼ inches.

295

304

October 12

338. Head. Pencil and ink on white paper, 35⅜ x 23 inches.

October 13

339. Head. Ink and oil on canvas, 21⅝ x 18⅛ inches.

October 17

340. Head. Oil on canvas, 36¼ x 28⅝ inches.

320

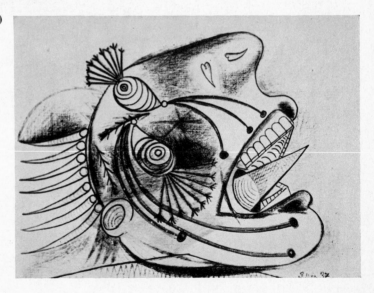

280 (detail)

341

341. Birdcage and Playing Cards. 1937(dated). Oil, 32 x 23¾ inches. Lent by Mme. Elsa
Schiaparelli. A continuation of the still life series begun before Guernica late in 1936
(nos. 276-78).

342. Portrait of a Lady. 1937(dated on back). Oil, 36¼ x 25½ inches. Lent by the artist.

342

343

343. Portrait of Nusch. August 3, 1937(dated). Pen and ink wash. Lent by Roland Penrose. Inscribed: *Pour Nusch, pour Nusch, Picasso.*

"Nusch" is the wife of the poet, Paul Eluard, a friend of Picasso's and at the time of this drawing the chief personal link between him and the Surrealist Movement. The Surrealists, Man Ray, whose great photograph of Picasso is reproduced on page 14, and André Breton, whose portrait Picasso etched as early as 1923 (bibl. 91, no. 110), have also been his friends. While they acclaim him as the greatest Surrealist artist and while he has participated in Surrealist exhibitions and books, he has never been officially a member of the group.

344. The End of a Monster. Paris, December 6, 1937 (dated). Pencil, 15⅛ x 22¼ inches. Lent by Roland Penrose.

345. Girl with a Cock. Paris, February 15, 1938(dated on back). Oil, 57¼ x 47½ inches. Lent by Mrs. Meric Callery.

Picasso's most important work of 1938.

344

345

346

346. Cock. Paris, March 29, 1938(dated). Pastel, 30½ x 22¼ inches. Lent anonymously.

347. Cock. Paris, March 23, 1938(dated). Charcoal, 30⅛ x 21¾ inches. Lent by Pierre Loeb.

348. Cock. March 29, 1938(dated). Pastel, 30¼ x 22⅛ inches. Lent by Walter P. Chrysler, Jr.

349

349. Portrait. May 24, 1938(dated). Oil, 28½ x 24¼ inches. Lent by Walter P. Chrysler, Jr.

350. Head of a Woman. Paris, April 27, 1938(dated). Color crayon, 30⅛ x 21¾ inches. Lent by Mrs. Meric Callery. Illustrated bibl. 40, p. 143.

351. Seated Woman. April 28, 1938 (dated). Ink, 30 x 21¾ inches. Lent by Mrs. Meric Callery. Illustrated bibl. 40, p. 142.

352. Woman in an Armchair. Paris, April 29, 1938 (dated). Color crayon over ink wash, 30⅛ x 21¾ inches. Lent by Mrs. Meric Callery.

353. Woman in an Armchair. Paris, July 4, 1938 (dated). Ink and crayon, 25½ x 19¾ inches. Lent by Mrs. Meric Callery. Illustrated bibl. 40, p. 157.

354. Three Figures. Mougins, August 10, 1938 (dated). Ink and wash, 17⅝ x 26¾ inches. Lent by Mrs. Meric Callery. Illustrated bibl. 40, p. 176.

355. Man with an All-day-sucker. August 20, 1938 (dated). Oil, 26⅞ x 18 inches. Lent by Walter P. Chrysler, Jr.

356. Girl in a Straw Hat. Mougins, August 29, 1938 (dated). Oil, 25⅝ x 19¾ inches. Lent by Lee A. Ault. Illustrated bibl. 40, p. 184.

357. Head of a Woman. Mougins, September 8, 1938 (dated). Ink, 26¾ x 17⅝ inches. Lent by Mrs. Meric Callery.

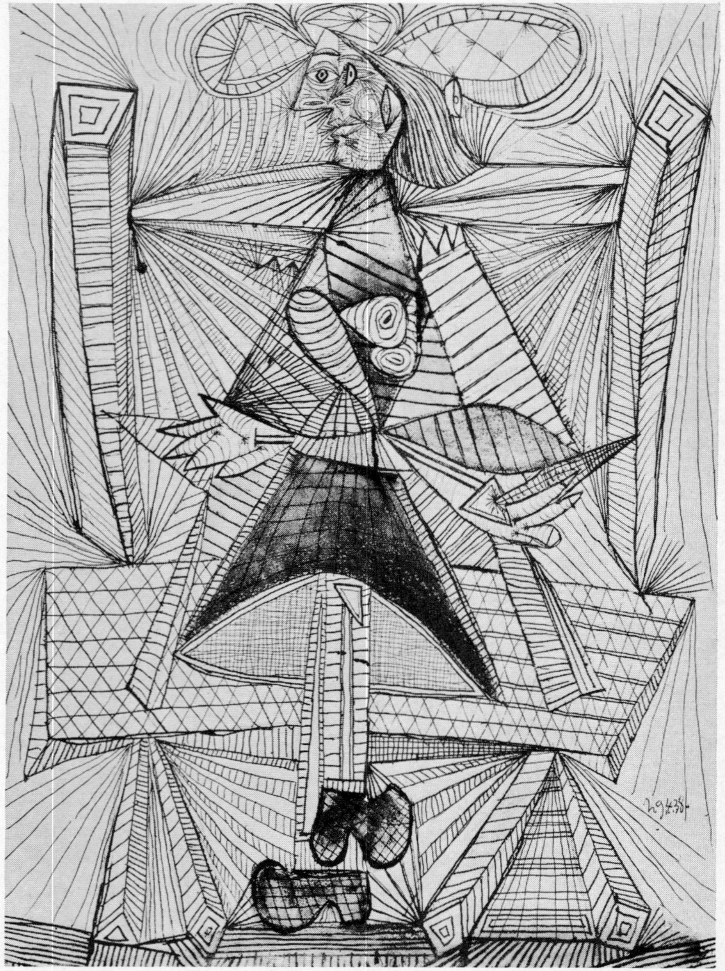

352

357

355

359

358. Still Life with a Bull's Skull. January 15, 1939(dated). Oil. Lent anonymously. Illustrated bibl. 225, p. 88.

359. Girl with Dark Hair. Paris, March 29, 1939(dated). Oil on wood, 23¾ x 17⅞ inches. Lent by Rosenberg and Helft Ltd.

360. Girl with Blond Hair. Paris, March 28, 1939(dated). Oil on wood, 23¾ x 17¾ inches. Lent by Rosenberg and Helft Ltd.

360a. Inspiration. Gobelin tapestry, 1935? 76 x 68½ inches. Designed by Picasso, 1934 (dated).

360b. Minotaur. Gobelin tapestry, 1936, 56½ x 93 inches. After a design by Picasso, a composition in pasted paper and paint on paper, 54¾ x 90⅝ inches, dated January 1928. Compare the painting of a similar subject, no. 213. Lent through the courtesy of Mme. Cuttoli, Miss Dorothy Liebes and the San Francisco Museum of Art.

Ballets in which Picasso collaborated

Picasso was active as a designer for the ballet from early in 1917 until 1924. No effort has been made to bring together all his ballet designs in this exhibition but some half dozen original pieces are included. These are supplemented by reproductions, posters, programs illustrated by Picasso, and also by numerous original drawings of ballet dancers and of Sergei Diaghilev, the great impresario of the Russian Ballet (see nos. 130, 132, 137, 194, 195, 196, 197). All the ballets listed were originally produced by Diaghilev except Mercure. The following data have been prepared by Paul Magriel, special librarian in charge of the American Dance Archives.

PARADE

Ballet in one act. Book: Jean Cocteau. Music: Eric Satie. Choreography: Léonide Massine. Curtain, scenery and costumes: Pablo Picasso. First produced: Théâtre du Châtelet, Paris, May 18, 1917.

The design for the Chinese Conjurer's costume, worn by Massine in the original production, is the gouache in this exhibition, no. 129, illustrated.

LE TRICORNE

Ballet in one act. Book: Martinez Sierra. Music: Manuel de Falla. Choreography: Léonide Massine. Scenery and costumes: Pablo Picasso. First produced: Alhambra Theatre, London, July 22, 1919.

An oil study for the curtain is included in this exhibition, no. 135; the gouaches nos. 134, 136 are possibly costume studies. A portfolio of color reproductions of designs for Le Tricorne, Paris, Paul Rosenberg, 1920, is also included.

PULCINELLA

Ballet in one act. Music: Igor Stravinsky (after Pergolesi). Choreography: Léonide Massine. Curtain, scenery and costumes: Pablo Picasso. First produced: Théâtre National de l'Opéra, Paris, May 15, 1920.

Costume designs, possibly for Pulcinella, are included in this exhibition, nos. 133 and 137.

CUADRO FLAMENCO

Suite of Andalusian dances. Folk music arranged by Manuel de Falla. Scenery and costumes: Pablo Picasso, made at the house of Jove, Paris, under the direction of Mme. Bongard. First produced: Paris, Théâtre de la Gaîté-Lyrique, May 22, 1921.

A section of the scenery representing a theatre box is included in the exhibition, no. 138, illustrated.

MERCURE

Poses plastiques. Choreography: Léonide Massine. Music: Eric Satie. Scenery and Costumes: Pablo Picasso. First produced: Paris, June 15, 1924; Soirées de Paris, for Comte Etienne de Beaumont.

LE TRAIN BLEU

Ballet in one act. Book: Jean Cocteau. Music: Darius Milhaud. Scenery: H. Laurens. Costumes: Chanel. Curtain: Pablo Picasso. Choreography: Bronia Nijinsky. First produced: Théâtre des Champs-Elysées, Paris, June 20, 1924.

The curtain was an enlargement of the gouache, The Race, 1922, reproduced in color in the frontispiece, no. 167.

Books illustrated by Picasso

Strictly speaking, a book should not be called illustrated unless the artist's contribution has been made with reference to the literary subject matter. In this sense, only a few volumes in this exhibition are "illustrated"; but two of them — Balzac's Le chef-d'oeuvre inconnu and Ovid's Les métamorphoses — rank among the finest works in the entire history of book illustration. It will be seen, however, that many of the volumes here listed comprise verse or prose by Picasso's friends to whom he has obligingly presented a print or drawing.

Many paintings and drawings by Picasso are reproduced in ballet programs. M. W.

1905 SALMON, André. Poëmes, Paris, Vers et Prose. 10(?) copies on Japan and Holland paper contain 1 drypoint. G. 6.

1911 JACOB, Max. Saint-Matorel. Paris, Kahnweiler. Contains 4 etchings. G. 23-26. (Catalog no. 93.)

1913 APOLLINAIRE, Guillaume. Alcools. Paris, Mercure de France. Contains reproduction of 1 portrait drawing of the author.

1914 JACOB, Max. Le siège de Jérusalem. Paris, Kahnweiler. Contains 3 etchings and drypoints. G. 35-37. (Catalog no. 121.)

1917 JACOB, Max. Le phanérogame. Paris, published by the author. 20 copies on old Japan contain 1 zinc etching. G. 55.

1917 JACOB, Max. Le cornet à dés. Paris, published by the author. Contains 1 burin engraving. G. 54.

1919 JACOB, Max. La défense de Tartuffe. Paris, Société Littéraire de France. 14 copies contain 1 burin engraving. G. 54.

1919 SALMON, André. Le manuscrit trouvé dans un chapeau. Paris, Société Littéraire de France. Contains reproductions of 38 drawings.

1921 VALERY, Paul. La jeune parque. Paris, N.R.F. 525 copies contain 1 portrait transfer-lithograph by Picasso. G. 224.

1921 SALMON, André. Peindre. Paris, La Sirène. Contains reproduction of 1 portrait drawing of the author.

1922 REVERDY, Pierre. Cravates de chanvre. Paris, Nord-Sud. 132 copies on Japan and Holland paper contain 3 etchings. G. 63-65.

1923 BRETON, André. Clair de terre. Paris, published by the author. 40 large-paper copies contain an original drypoint portrait etching of the author, the others a reproduction. G. 110.

1925 RADIGUET, Raymond. Les joues en feu. Paris. Contains reproduction of 1 portrait drawing of the author. G. 223.

1926 GEORGE, Waldemar. Picasso dessins. Paris, Quatre Chemins. 100 copies on Arches contain 1 lithograph. G. 240.

1930 STEIN, Gertrude. Dix portraits. Paris, La Montaigne. 100 copies on large-paper contain reproductions of drawings by Picasso (3); Tchelitchew (1); Bérard (2); Tonny (2); Berman (2).

1931 OVID. Les métamorphoses. Lausanne, Skira. Contains 30 etchings. G. 143-72. (See no. 226 for reproduction.)

1931 BALZAC, Honoré. Le chef-d'oeuvre inconnu. Paris, Vollard. Contains 13 etchings and 124 wood-engravings by Aubert, after drawings by Picasso. G. 123-35. (See nos. 205 and 206 for reproductions.)

1934 LEVINSON, André. Serge Lifar. Paris, Grasset. Contains 1 drawing.

1934 ARISTOPHANES. Lysistrata, a new version by Gilbert Seldes. New York, Limited Editions Club. Contains 6 etchings and reproductions of 33 drawings by Picasso. (See no. 270 for reproduction.)

1936 ELUARD, Paul. Les yeux fertiles. Paris, G.L.M. Contains 5 drawings, including a portrait of the author. 10 copies on Imperial Japan contain 1 etching.

Prints by Picasso in the exhibition

Catalog nos.: 26, 33, 34, 35, 36, 37, 38, 39, 40, 41, 42, 43, 44, 45, 46, 75, 85, 86, 93, 101, 102, 121, 123, 160, 175, 176, 177, 198, 202, 203, 205, 205a, 206, 222, 223, 225, 226, 227, 239, 251, 252, 253, 270, 272, 273, 274, 275, 333, 334.

Works by Picasso in American museums and private collections open to the public

*A number in parentheses following an item indicates that it is included in this exhibition, and a star * that it is illustrated in this catalog. The list may not be complete. Prints are not included.*　　　　D. M.

BUFFALO, NEW YORK. BUFFALO FINE ARTS ACADEMY, ALBRIGHT ART GALLERY
　　　　　　La Toilette.　1905. Oil, 59½ x 39½ inches (no. *57)

CAMBRIDGE, MASSACHUSETTS. FOGG ART MUSEUM, HARVARD UNIVERSITY
　　　　　　Standing Nude Man.　1904. Ink (on back of next item)
　　　　　　Mother and Child.　1904. Crayon, 13½ x 10½ inches (no. *23)
　　　　　　Bathers.　1918. Pencil, 9⅛ x 12¼ inches (no. *142)
　　　　　　Philosopher.　1918? Pencil, 13⅝ x 10⁷⁄₁₆ inches (no. 143)
　　　　　　Pierrot.　Pencil, 34 x 22¼ inches
　　　　　　Reclining Bather.　1923. Drawing, 10¼ x 13¾ inches

CHICAGO. ART INSTITUTE OF CHICAGO
　　　　　　On the Upper Deck.　1901. Oil, 15½ x 24¼ inches (no. *9)
　　　　　　The Old Guitarist.　1903. Oil on panel, 47¾ x 32½ inches (no. *20)
　　　　　　Au Cabaret.　Crayon, 4⅞ x 8¼ inches
　　　　　　Girl and Man.　Ink, 9⅝ x 12⅝ inches
　　　　　　Nude Man.　Pencil, 12 x 8 inches
　　　　　　Peasants from Andorra.　1906? Ink, 22⅞ x 13½ inches (no. *63)
　　　　　　Musical Instruments.　1916. Gouache, 5¾ x 4⅝ inches

CHICAGO. ARTS CLUB OF CHICAGO
　　　　　　Head of Woman.　1923. Red chalk, 23½ x 17½ inches

CLEVELAND, OHIO. CLEVELAND MUSEUM OF ART
　　　　　　Standing Nude.　1905. Gouache, 25¼ x 19¼ inches (no. *61)

COLUMBUS, OHIO. COLUMBUS GALLERY OF FINE ARTS
　　　　　　The Appetizer.　1901. Watercolor, 17 x 13½ inches
　　　　　　Boy with Cattle.　1903-04. Gouache, 23½ x 18½ inches
　　　　　　Portrait with words "J'aime Eva."　1912. Oil, 38¾ x 25 inches (no. *109)
　　　　　　Still Life.　1915. Oil, 25 x 31½ inches
　　　　　　Abstraction.　1916. Watercolor, 17½ x 13¼ inches

DETROIT, MICHIGAN. DETROIT INSTITUTE OF FINE ARTS
　　　　　　Portrait of E. Forert.　Charcoal

HARTFORD, CONNECTICUT. WADSWORTH ATHENEUM
　　　　　　Standing Nude.　1922. Oil on wood, 7½ x 5½ inches (no. *169)
　　　　　　Two Ballet Dancers Resting.　1925. Ink, 13½ x 9¾ inches (no. 196)

HONOLULU, HAWAII. ACADEMY OF ARTS
　　　　　　Pierrot.　1927. Oil, 22 x 18 inches

LOS ANGELES, CALIFORNIA. LOS ANGELES MUSEUM
　　　　　　Figure.　1912-13. Charcoal and ink?
　　　　　　Woman at Mirror.　1934. Watercolor

MERION, PENNSYLVANIA. BARNES FOUNDATION

> Girl with Cigarette. 1901. Oil
> The Baby. 1901. Oil
> Peasants (Composition). 1905. Oil
> Acrobats. 1905. Oil
> Still Life. 1915? Oil

NEW YORK. MUSEUM OF LIVING ART, NEW YORK UNIVERSITY

> Self Portrait. 1906. Oil, 36 x 28 inches (no. *66)
> Composition study for *Les Demoiselles d'Avignon*. 1907 .Watercolor, $6\frac{3}{4}$ x $8\frac{3}{4}$ inches (no. *70)
> Bowls and Jug. 1908. Oil, 32 x $25\frac{1}{2}$ inches (no. *79)
> Pipe and Violin. 1911. Oil, $22\frac{1}{2}$ x 18 inches
> Drawing. 1912. Charcoal, 18 x 23 inches
> Still Life with Fruit. 1913. Pasted paper and charcoal, $25\frac{1}{2}$ x $19\frac{1}{2}$ inches (no. 112)
> Guitar and Bottle. 1913. Pencil, 12 x $15\frac{3}{4}$ inches
> Composition. 1914. Watercolor and pencil, $7\frac{1}{2}$ x $11\frac{1}{4}$ inches
> Still Life. 1914. Oil, 12 x $16\frac{1}{4}$ inches
> Glass of Absinthe. 1914. Painted bronze, $8\frac{3}{4}$ inches high (no. *119)
> Open Window. 1919. Watercolor, $13\frac{1}{4}$ x $8\frac{3}{4}$ inches
> Three Musicians. 1921. Oil, 80 x 74 inches (no. *165)
> Composition. 1922. Oil, $6\frac{1}{4}$ x $8\frac{1}{2}$ inches
> Still Life. 1923. Oil, 32 x $29\frac{1}{2}$ inches
> Still Life. 1924. Conté crayon with oil wash, $9\frac{1}{4}$ x $6\frac{3}{4}$ inches (no. 183)
> Composition. 1926. Ink and pastel, $12\frac{1}{4}$ x $18\frac{1}{4}$ inches
> Dinard. 1928. Oil, $9\frac{1}{2}$ x $6\frac{1}{2}$ inches
> Study for *Lysistrata* illustrations. 1934. Ink, $9\frac{1}{2}$ x $13\frac{3}{4}$ inches (no. 271)

NEW YORK. MUSEUM OF MODERN ART

> La Coiffure. 1905. Oil, $68\frac{7}{8}$ x $39\frac{1}{4}$ inches (no. 51)
> Hercules. 1905? Ink, $6\frac{3}{4}$ x $4\frac{1}{4}$ inches
> Les Demoiselles d'Avignon. 1906-07. Oil, 96 x 92 inches (no. *71)
> Head. 1909. Gouache, 24 x 18 inches (no. 88)
> Man with a Hat. 1913. Papier collé, charcoal, ink, $24\frac{1}{2}$ x $18\frac{1}{4}$ inches (no. 105)
> Green Still Life. 1914. Oil, $23\frac{1}{2}$ x $31\frac{1}{4}$ inches (no. 120)
> Seated Woman. 1918. Gouache, $5\frac{1}{2}$ x $4\frac{1}{2}$ inches
> Woman in White. 1923. Oil, 39 x $31\frac{1}{2}$ inches (no. *179)
> Four Ballet Dancers. 1925. Ink, $13\frac{1}{2}$ x 10 inches (no. *195)
> Guitar and Fruit. 1924? Oil, $51\frac{1}{4}$ x $38\frac{1}{4}$ inches
> Seated Woman. 1926-27. Oil, $51\frac{1}{2}$ x $38\frac{1}{2}$ inches (no. *208)
> The Studio. 1927-28. Oil, 59 x 91 inches (no. *212)
> Girl before a Mirror. 1932. Oil, $63\frac{3}{4}$ x $51\frac{1}{4}$ inches (no. *246)

NEW YORK. BROOKLYN MUSEUM

> Head of a Young Man. 1923? Crayon, $24\frac{1}{2}$ x $18\frac{3}{4}$ inches (no. 178)

NEW YORK. SOLOMON R. GUGGENHEIM FOUNDATION

> Fruit Bowl. 1908. Oil, $25\frac{3}{8}$ x $28\frac{1}{4}$ inches
> Pierrot (Seated Man). 1911. Oil, $51\frac{1}{4}$ x $35\frac{1}{8}$ inches (no. *97)
> Landscape, Céret. 1914. Oil, $25\frac{1}{2}$ x $19\frac{3}{4}$ inches
> Musician. 1914. Oil, 25 x $19\frac{1}{2}$ inches

Abstraction. 1916. Collage, 18½ x 24½ inches
Abstraction. 1918. Oil, 14 x 11 inches
Composition. 1918. Oil, 13½ x 10½ inches
Lemon. 1927. Oil, 7 x 5¼ inches

NEW YORK. CHESTER DALE COLLECTION (OPEN BY APPOINTMENT ONLY)
The Gourmet. 1901. Oil, 36 x 27 inches
The Tragedy. 1903. Oil on panel, 41½ x 27¼ inches
Study for the *Juggler*. 1905? Drawing, 10¼ x 7¼ inches
Juggler with Still Life. 1905. Oil on cardboard, 38¾ x 27¼ inches
Two Youths. 1905. Oil, 59¼ x 36¾ inches
The Acrobat's Family. 1905. Oil, 92½ x 87½ inches
Still Life, Mandolin. 1918. Oil, 38 x 51¼ inches
Classical Head. 1922. Oil, 24 x 19¾ inches
Portrait of Mme. Picasso. 1923. Oil, 39½ x 32 inches
The Lovers. 1923. Oil, 50 x 38 inches

NORTHAMPTON, MASSACHUSETTS. SMITH COLLEGE MUSEUM OF ART
The Table. 1919-20. Oil, 51 x 29⅝ inches (no. *147)

PHILADELPHIA. PHILADELPHIA MUSEUM OF ART
Woman with Loaves. 1905. Oil, 39 x 27½ inches (no. *56)

PROVIDENCE, RHODE ISLAND. MUSEUM OF THE RHODE ISLAND SCHOOL OF DESIGN
La Vie. 1903. Oil, 77⅜ x 50⅞ inches (no. *19)
Two Nudes. 1923. Ink

ROCHESTER, NEW YORK. MEMORIAL ART GALLERY
Flowers in a Blue Vase. 1904? Gouache, 24¼ x 18½ inches

ST. LOUIS, MISSOURI. CITY ART MUSEUM
The Mother. 1901. Canvas on cardboard, 29½ x 20 inches
Nude. 1907. Oil on panel, 13⅞ x 8½ inches

TOLEDO, OHIO. TOLEDO MUSEUM OF ART
Woman with a Crow. 1904. Gouache and pastel, 25⅝ x 19⅛ inches (no. *25)
Head of a Woman. 1905. Gouache, 25⅛ x 19 inches

WASHINGTON, D. C. PHILLIPS MEMORIAL GALLERY
The Blue Room. 1901. Oil, 20 x 24½ inches (no. *15)
Jester. 1905. Bronze, 16¼ inches high (no. *32)
Woman. 1918. Oil, 13¾ x 10½ inches
Studio Corner. 1921. Watercolor, 8 x 10¼ inches
Bull Fight. 1934. Oil, 19¾ x 25¾ inches (no. *263)

Where Picasso has lived: a chronology

For the years 1881-1906 Christian Zervos' introduction to Volume I of his catalogue raisonné of Picasso's work (bibl. 231) is the principal authority. For subsequent years a list especially prepared by Henry Kahnweiler has proved indispensable.

A. H. B. Jr.

1881   October 25th. Born in Malaga, Spain.

1891   Moves with parents to Corunna.

1895   Moves with parents to Barcelona.

1896-1900   Barcelona, Madrid, Barcelona.

1900   Paris (October, for a month — 49 rue Gabrielle).

1901   Malaga, Madrid, Paris (spring — 130ter Boulevard de Clichy), Barcelona.

1902   Barcelona (8 months), Paris (autumn — Hotel Champollion, rue Champollion; Hotel du Maroc, rue de Seine; Boulevard Barbès).

1903   Barcelona.

1904   Paris (spring — 13 rue Ravignan, now 13 Place Emile-Goudeau, where he lived until 1909).

	PARIS ADDRESSES	SUMMER VACATIONS AND OTHER EXCURSIONS
1905	13 rue Ravignan	Holland (summer, a few weeks). Gosol, Andorra Valley, Spanish Pyrenees (end of 1905, early 1906).
1906	" " "	Gosol (summer).
1907	" " "	Avignon?
1908	" " "	La Rue des Bois (Oise) (a few weeks, summer).
1909	From 13 rue de Ravignan to . . . . . 11 Boulevard de Clichy	Horta on the Ebro, Spain.
1910	" " " "	Cadaqués, Spain.
1911	" " " "	Céret, French Pyrenees.
1912	From 11 Boulevard de Clichy to . . . . 242 Boulevard Raspail	Sorgues sur l'Ouvèze (Vaucluse).
1913	To 5bis rue Schoelcher	Céret, French Pyrenees.
1914	" " "	Avignon (until August, then Paris).
1915	" " "	
1916	To 22 rue Victor Hugo, Montrouge (Seine) .	
1917	" " " "	Rome, Naples, Florence (February for a month) Madrid, Barcelona (summer).
1918	From Montrouge to . . . . . . 23 rue la Böétie (October)	Biarritz.
1919	" " "	St. Raphaël (Var).
1920	" " "	Juan les Pins.
1921	" " "	Fontainebleau.
1922	" " "	Dinard.
1923	" " "	Cap d'Antibes (A.M.).
1924	" " "	Juan les Pins.
1925	" " "	" " "

WHERE PICASSO HAS LIVED

	PARIS ADDRESSES	SUMMER VACATIONS AND OTHER EXCURSIONS
1926	23 rue la Böétie	Juan les Pins.
1927	" " "	Cannes.
1928	" " "	Dinard.
1929	" " "	"
1930	" " "	Juan les Pins.
1931	" " "	" " "
1932	" " "	buys Château du Boisgeloup at Gisors (Eure).
1933	" " "	Cannes, Barcelona
1934	" " "	Boisgeloup, San Sebastian, Madrid, Toledo, Escorial, Barcelona.
1935	" " "	Boisgeloup.
1936	" " "	Mougins (A.M.).
1937	" " "	"
1938	takes studio, 7 rue des Grands Augustins, but lives at 23 rue la Böétie	"
1939	" " "	Antibes. October, near Bordeaux.

Exhibitions of Picasso's work

Reprinted from Bazin (bibl 24), with additions and corrections

1897 BARCELONA. Reviewed by Cadalo, bibl 37

1901 PARIS, Ambroise Vollard Gallery. With Iturrino. Reviewed by Fagus, bibl 78

1902 PARIS, B. Weill Gallery. Catalog preface by Farge, bibl 79

1902 PARIS, Ambroise Vollard Gallery

1909 PARIS, Ambroise Vollard Gallery

1911 NEW YORK, Photo-Secession Gallery. Catalog preface by De Zayas, bibl 67

1912 BARCELONA, Dalmau Gallery

1912 COLOGNE, special room in the Sonderbund exhibition

1912 LONDON, Stafford Gallery

1913 BERLIN, Neue Galerie

1913 BERLIN, Sezession Galerie

1913 COLOGNE, Rheinische Kunstsalon

1913 MUNICH, Moderne Galerie Thannhauser

1914 BERLIN, Neue Galerie

1914 DRESDEN, E. Richter Gallery

1914 MUNICH, Caspari Gallery

1914-15 NEW YORK, Photo-Secession Gallery

1919 PARIS, Galerie de l'Effort Moderne (Léonce Rosenberg)

1919 PARIS, Paul Rosenberg Gallery

1920 PARIS, Paul Rosenberg Gallery

1920 ROME, Valori Plastici Gallery

1921 LONDON, Leicester Galleries. Catalog, bibl 125

1921 PARIS, Paul Rosenberg Gallery

1922 MUNICH, Moderne Galerie Thannhauser

1923 CHICAGO, Arts Club. Drawings. Catalog, bibl 17

1923 PRAGUE, Mánes Art Society

1924 PARIS, Paul Rosenberg Gallery

1926 PARIS, Paul Rosenberg Gallery

1927 BERLIN, Galerie Alfred Flechtheim. Catalog, bibl 84

1927 PARIS, Paul Rosenberg Gallery

1928 CHICAGO, Arts Club. Drawings. Catalog, bibl 16

1928 PARIS, Galerie Pierre

1930 CHICAGO, Arts Club. Catalog, bibl 18

1930 NEW YORK, John Becker Gallery. Drawings and gouaches. Catalog, bibl 25

1930 NEW YORK, Reinhardt Gallery. With Derain. Catalog, bibl 177

1930 PARIS, M. G. Aron Gallery

1931 CAMBRIDGE, Mass. Harvard Society for Contemporary Art. Catalog, bibl 111

1931 LONDON, Alex. Reid & Lefevre, Ltd. Catalog, bibl 176

1931 NEW YORK, Demotte, Inc.

1931 NEW YORK, Marie Harriman Gallery. Ovid illustrations

1931 NEW YORK, Valentine Gallery. Catalog, bibl 211

1931 PARIS, Percier Gallery

1931 PARIS, Paul Rosenberg Gallery

1931 CAMBRIDGE, MASSACHUSETTS, Harvard Society for Contemporary Art. Catalog, bibl 111

1932 CAMBRIDGE, MASSACHUSETTS, Harvard Society for Contemporary Art. Ovid illustrations. Catalog, bibl 110

1932 HANNOVER, Kestner-Gesellschaft. With Schlemmer. Catalog, bibl 108

1932 MUNICH, Das Graphische Kabinett. Ovid illustrations

1932 PARIS, Georges Petit Gallery. Catalog, bibl 154

1932 ZURICH, Kunsthaus. Catalog, bibl 237

1933 NEW YORK, Valentine Gallery. Catalog, bibl 212

1934 HARTFORD, CONN., Wadsworth Atheneum. Catalog, bibl 109

1935 PARIS, Percier Gallery. Papiers collés 1912-1914. Catalog, bibl 160

1936 LONDON, Zwemmer Gallery

1936 MADRID, Amigos de las Artes Nuevas. Cat bibl 9

1936 NEW YORK, Jacques Seligmann & Co. Cat bibl 197

1936 PARIS, Cahiers d'Art Gallery. Sculpture

1936 PARIS, Renou & Colle Gallery

1936 PARIS, Paul Rosenberg Gallery. Catalog, bibl 185

1937 CHICAGO, Arts Club

1937 LONDON, Zwemmer Gallery. Catalog, bibl 238

1937 NEW YORK, Jacques Seligmann & Co. Cat bibl 198

1937 NEW YORK, Valentine Gallery. Catalog, bibl 213

1937 PARIS, Kate Perls Gallery. Catalog, bibl 153

1938 BOSTON, Museum of Modern Art. With Matisse. Catalog, bibl 33

1938 LONDON, London Gallery. Drawings and collages

1938 LONDON, New Burlington Galleries. Guernica

1938 NEW YORK, Valentine Gallery. Catalog, bibl 214

1939 CHICAGO, Arts Club. Drawings

1939 LONDON, Rosenberg & Helft Gallery. Catalog, bibl 183

1939 LONDON, London Gallery. Catalog in bibl 129

1939 LOS ANGELES, Stendahl Art Galleries. Guernica

1939 NEW YORK, Valentine Gallery. Guernica

1939 NEW YORK, Westermann Gallery. Prints

1939 NEW YORK, Perls Galleries. Catalog, bibl 152

1939 PARIS, Paul Rosenberg Gallery. Catalog, bibl 184

1939 NEW YORK, Museum of Modern Art

1940 CHICAGO, Art Institute

Bibliography

This bibliography is based on those of Bazin (24), Grohmann (104), Torre (87) and Scheiwiller (232). The work of these bibliographers has been edited to eliminate inconsistencies due to the duplicate entry of translations and reprints, and many minor references listed by them have been omitted. A great deal of new material has been added, and the bibliography has been brought up to date. Every reference, with the exception of the six marked †, has been checked with the original.

The arrangement is alphabetical, under the author's name wherever possible. Catalogs of exhibitions in public museums are listed under the name of the city where the museum is located, while private exhibition galleries are listed under the name of the gallery.

The bibliographical form is modelled upon that used by the Art Index. Special thanks are due to Miss Sarah St. John, Editor of the Art Index, for criticizing and proofreading the manuscript.

ABBREVIATIONS. Ap *April,* Ag *August,* col *color(ed),* D *December,* ed *editor,* -ion, F *February,* il *illustration(s),* Ja *January,* Je *June,* Jl *July,* Mr *March,* My *May,* N *November,* no *number,* ns *new series,* O *October,* p *page(s),* pseud *pseudonym,* S *September.* * in the Museum of Modern Art Library. † not seen by the compiler, but listed because of its inclusion in a reliable bibliography.

SAMPLE ENTRY for magazine article. GRAHAM, J. D. Primitive art and Picasso. 8il Magazine of Art 30:236-9 Ap 1937.

EXPLANATION. An article by J. D. Graham, entitled "Primitive Art and Picasso," containing 8 illustrations, will be found in the Magazine of Art, volume 30, pages 236 to 239 inclusive, the April, 1937 issue.

BEAUMONT NEWHALL

STATEMENTS BY PICASSO

* 1 PICASSO SPEAKS. The Arts 3:315-26 My 1923
    Forbes Watson, former editor of The Arts states (1939) that this interview was given in Spanish to Marius De Zayas, and that Picasso approved the manuscript before its translation
* into English. This interview is reprinted in Picasso, 2 statements, New York, Los Angeles, Armitage, 1936, p3-21. A French version, with additional paragraphs dealing with "Douanier" Rousseau, negro art, and literature, appeared in
* Florent Fels, Propos d'artistes, Paris, Renaissance du Livre, 1925, p 139-45. German translations are to be found in Weltkunst no 16 1930, and in Paul Westheim, Künstlerbekentnisse, Berlin, Propyläen-Verlag, 1925, p 144-7. A Czech version is in Volné Směry 24:27-8 1925-26.

Reprinted in this volume, page 9

2 [LETTER ON ART] Ogoniok (Moscow) no20 My 16 1926
    Published without indication of source. Picasso says (1939) that the letter is spurious. It has been republished in the
* following: Formes no2:2-5 1930; Deutsche Kunst und Dekor-
* ation 58:277-84 1926; Creative Art 6:383-5 Je 1930; Picasso,
* 2 statements, New York, Los Angeles, Armitage, 1936, p23-49; Europe, an American Monthly F 1936.

* 3 CONVERSATION AVEC PICASSO. Cahiers d'Art 10:173-8 1935
* English translation in M. Evans, ed, The painter's object,
* London, Howe, 1937, p81-8. Spanish translation in Gaceta de Arte (Tenerife) ns no37:10-13 Mr 1936.

Reprinted in this volume, page 13

POETRY BY PICASSO
* 4 CAHIERS D'ART 10:185-91, 225-38 1935
    Commentary by André Breton and J. Sabartés. Two of these poems are reprinted in Gaceta de Arte (Tenerife) ns no37:17-19 1936.

4a CAHIERS D'ART 13no3-10:156-7 1938
    Facsimile of a manuscript.

4b CONTEMPORARY POETRY AND PROSE (LONDON) 1no 4-5 Ag-S 1936
    "Picasso Poems Number." 6 poems translated by George Reavy.

* 5 LONDON BULLETIN no 15-16 My 15 1939
    With English translation.

* 6 SUEÑO Y MENTIRA DE FRANCO. [Paris] 1937
    Facsimile of manuscript, Spanish transcription, French translation. Published in folio with proofs of the etchings. English translation inserted.

LITERATURE ON PICASSO
* 7 ABBOTT, JERE. An abstract painting by Picasso [La table, 1920] 5il Bulletin of the Smith College Museum of Art no 14:1-6 My 1933

* 8 AKSENOV, IVAN ALEKSANDROVICH. Picasso i okrestnosti. 64p 12il Moscow, Tzentrifuga, 1917
    Text dated June 1914.

* 9 AMIGOS DE LAS ARTES NUEVAS, MADRID. Picasso. 16p 7il 1936
    Exhibition catalog.

* 10 APOLLINAIRE, GUILLAUME. Il y a. p 199-200 Paris, Messein, 1925
    Poem, "Pablo Picasso."

* 11 —— Les peintres cubistes. 9e éd. p31-9 Paris, Figuière, 1913
* English translation of the pages on Picasso in Little Review 9:41-6 Autumn 1922.

12 —— Picasso et les papiers collés. Montjoie (Paris) p6 Mr 14 1913
* Reprinted in Cahiers d'Art 7no3-5:117 1932.

* 13 ARAGON, LOUIS. La peinture au défi. p 11-12 3il Paris, Corti, 1930
    Introduction to an exhibition of collages at the Galerie Goemans, Paris.

14 ARP, HANS AND NEITZEL, L. H. Neue französische malerei. p9-10 4il Leipzig, Verlag der Weissen Bücher, 1913

* 15 ART'S ACROBAT. col il Time 33no7:44-6 F 13 1939
On cover: color photograph of Picasso by Dora Maar.

16 ARTS CLUB OF CHICAGO. Catalogue of an exhibition of original drawings by Picasso, loaned by Wildenstein & Co. 1928

17 —— Catalogue of an exhibition of original drawings by Picasso. 6p il 1923

* 18 —— Paintings by Picasso, catalog of an exhibition. 2p il 1930

* 19 BARNES, ALBERT C. The art in painting. 2d ed. p389-93, 537-9 4il New York, Harcourt, Brace, 1928

* 20 BARR, ALFRED H., JR. Cubism and abstract art. p29-42, 78-92, 96-110 26il New York, Museum of Modern Art, 1936

21 BASLER, ADOLPHE. Fünfzehn jahre lügen. 3il Kunst und Künstler 26:143-7 1928

22 —— Pablo Picasso und der kubismus. 5il Der Cicerone 13:237-44 1921
* Reprinted in Jahrbuch der Jungen Kunst 2:153-60 1921.

23 B, G. Un bilan: l'exposition Picasso [à la galerie Georges Petit] 4il Amour de l'Art 13:246-7 1932

* 24 BAZIN, GERMAIN. Pablo Picasso. In R. Huyghe, ed. Histoire de l'art contemporain; la peinture. p221-6 Paris, Alcan, 1935
Bibliography.

* 25 BECKER, JOHN [ART DEALER] NEW YORK. Drawings and gouaches by Pablo Picasso. il [1930]
Exhibition catalog. Foreword by Frank Crowninshield.

25a BECKER, JOHN, PUBLISHER. Dix reproductions [des oeuvres de Picasso] 10 col il New York, 1933

26 BELL, CLIVE. Picasso: aesthetic truth and futurist nonsense. Outlook 137:20-3 My 7 1924

27 —— Picasso's mind. New Statesman and Nation 11:857-8 My 30 1936
* Reprinted in Living Age 350:532-4 Ag 1936.

28 —— Matisse and Picasso. The Athenaeum no 4698:643-4 My 14 1920
* Reprinted in 125, below. A revised version appeared in the New Republic 22:379-80 My 19 1920; in Arts and Decoration
* 14:42,44 1920; and in the author's Since Cézanne p83-90 London, Chatto and Windus, 1922.

29 BENET, RAFAEL. Picasso i Barcelona. 24il Art (Barcelona) p3-13 O 1933

* 30 BERTRAM, ANTHONY. Pablo Picasso. 9p 24il New York, Studio, 1934

* 31 BEUCLER, A. Sur le précubisme de Picasso. 6il Formes no 14:59-61 1931

32 BISSIÈRE. L'exposition Picasso [à la galerie Rosenberg] 4il Amour de l'Art 2:209-12 1921

32a BLUNT, ANTHONY. Picasso unfrocked. Spectator 159:584 O 8 1937
Discussion by Herbert Read, William Coldstream, Roland Penrose and Dora Birtles in same 159:636, 687, 747, 804 O 15—N 5 1937.

33 BOSTON MUSEUM OF MODERN ART. Picasso; Henri-Matisse. 4p 1938
Exhibition catalog.

* 34 BRETON, ANDRÉ. Picasso dans son élément. 59il Minotaure no 1:9-38 1933

* 35 —— Le surréalisme et la peinture. p 16-20 15il Paris, Editions de la Nouvelle Revue française, 1928

* 36 BRIAN, DORIS. The Picasso annual, 1938. 2il Art News 37:8, 19-20 N 12 1938

† 37 CADALO, RODRIGUEZ. Exposicion Ruiz Picasso. La Vanguardia (Barcelona) 1897

* 38 CAHIERS D'ART 7no3-5:85-196 1932
Special Picasso number, with 157 illustrations and text by Zervos, Salmon, Apollinaire, Strawinsky, Guéguen, Hugnet, Ramón Gómez de la Serna, Cocteau, J. J. Sweeney, H. S. Ede, Carl Einstein, Oskar Schürer, Will Grohmann, Maud Dale, Vicente Huidobro, Giovanni Scheiwiller, and others.

* 39 CAHIERS D'ART 10no7-10:145-261 1935
Special Picasso number, on works of years 1930-35, with 92 illustrations and text by Zervos, Eluard, Breton, Péret, Man Ray, Dali, Hugnet, Sabartés, Louis Fernandez, Juli González, Joan Miro.

* 39a CAHIERS D'ART 12no4-5:105-56 1937
Special Picasso issue, on his painting "Guernica," with 69 illustrations, and text by Zervos, Cassou, Duthuit, Mabille, Eluard, Leiris, Bergamin.

* 40 CAHIERS D'ART 13no3-10:73-80 1938
Special Picasso issue, with 120 illustrations, an article by Zervos, and a poem by Paul Eluard.

41 CAREW, KATE. Interviewing a cubist [Picasso] il Literary Digest 46:890-2 Ap 19 1913

42 CARRA, CARLO. Picasso. Valori Plastici (Rome) 2:101-7 1920
* French translation in Le Néoclassicisme dans l'art contemporain. p54-9 Rome, Valori Plastici, 1923.

43 CARTER, HUNTLY. The Plato-Picasso idea. il New Age ns 10:88 N 23 1911

44 CASSOU, JEAN. Derniers dessins de Picasso. 6il Cahiers d'Art 2:49-54 1927

* 45 —— Paysages de Picasso. 11 il Prométhée no3:35-42 Mr 1939

* 46 —— Picasso. 64p 62il Paris, Braun, 1937
Text in French, English and German.

47 —— Les solitudes de Picasso. 28il Renaissance de l'Art français 21:2-14, 49 Ja 1939
With English summary.

47a CENDRARS, BLAISE. Aujourd'hui. p 112-15 Paris, Grasset, 1931

48 CHARENSOL, G. Pablo Picasso. 6il Renaissance de l'Art français 15:142-6 Jl 1932

49 CHURCHILL, ALFRED VANCE. Picasso's failure. il Forum (New York) 73:776-83 Je 1925

50 COCTEAU, JEAN. Ode à Picasso. Paris, Bernouard, 1919
    Reprinted in the author's Poésie 1916-1919 p281-8 Paris, Gallimard, 1927; also in his Morceaux choisis. p65-72 Paris, Gallimard, 1932.

* 51 —— Picasso, 32p 16 il Paris, Stock, 1923
    Reprinted in the author's Le rappel à l'ordre p273-96 Paris, Stock, 1926. English translation: A call to order p223-48 New York, Holt [1927?]

52 —— Picasso, a fantastic modern genius. 4il Arts and Decoration 22:44, 72-4 D 1924

* 54 COGNIAT, RAYMOND. Décors de théâtre. 11 il Paris, Chroniques du Jour, 1930.
    List of ballets with décors by Picasso on unnumbered pages at end of book.

55 —— Picasso et la décoration théâtrale. 5il Amour de l'Art 9:299-302 1928

—— See also 77A

* 56 COQUIOT, GUSTAVE. Cubistes, futuristes, passéistes. p 145-50 il Paris, Ollendorf, 1914

* 57 —— Les indépendants. p 160-1 il Paris, Ollendorf [after 1920]

58 COSSIO DEL POMAR, FELIPE. Con los buscadores del camino. Gandhi, Rolland, Picasso, Papini, Unamuno, Ferrero, Bourdelle. p 105-32 Madrid, Ulises, 1932

59 COURTHION, PIERRE. Couleurs. p97-104 Paris, Editions des Cahiers Libres, 1926

* 60 COURVILLE, XAVIER DE. Les décors de Picasso aux Ballets russes. Revue Musicale 2:187-8 F 1921

* 61 CRAVEN, THOMAS. Modern art. p 177-92 2il New York, Simon and Schuster, 1934

* 62 —— Picasso waning? Art Digest 9:9 N 15 1934

* 63 CROWNINSHIELD, FRANK. The case of Pablo Picasso. col il Vogue (New York) p 108, 112 Je 1 1937

—— See also 25

* 64 DALE, MRS. MAUD. Picasso. 8p 62il New York, Knopf, 1930

* 65 DASBURG, ANDREW. Cubism—its rise and progress. 4il The Arts 4:278-84 N 1923

* 66 DAVIDSON, MARTHA. Second annual Picasso festival. 4il Art News 36:10-11, 22 N 6 1937

67 DE ZAYAS, MARIUS. Pablo Picasso. 1911
    A pamphlet, distributed at the Photo-Secession Gallery, New York, at the time of the first American Picasso exhibition.
*   Reprinted in Camera Work no35-36:65-7 1911.

—— See also 1

68 DESHAIRS, LÉON. Pablo Picasso. 12il Art et Décoration 47:73-84 1925

* 69 DOCUMENTS 2no3:113-84 1930
    Special Picasso issue, with 57 illustrations, and texts by Jacques Baron, Georges Bataille, Robert Desnos, Carl Einstein, Maurice Heine, Eugène Jolas, Marcel Jouhandeau, Edouard Kasyade, Michel Leiris, Camille Mauclair, Marcel Mauss, Georges Monnet, Léon Pierre-Quint, Jacques Prévert, Charles-Henri Puech, Dr. Reber, Georges Ribémont-Dessaignes, Georges Henri Rivière, André Schaeffner, Roger Vitrac. Notice documentaire, a chronology, p 180-2.

* 70 DODICI OPERE DI PICASSO. 12il Firenze, Libreria della Voce, 1914

* 71 EARP, T. W. The modern movement in painting. p28-34 2 col il London, Studio, 1935

72 —— The Picasso exhibition [at Alex. Reid & Lefevre galleries, London] 2il Apollo 14:40-2 1931

* 73 EINSTEIN, CARL. Die kunst des 20. jahrhunderts. 2. aufl. p68-87 41 il Berlin, Propyläen-Verlag, 1926

* 74 —— Pablo Picasso: quelques tableaux de 1928. 13il Documents 1:35-47 1929

75 —— Picasso, anlässlich der ausstellung in der galerie Georges Petit. 6il Weltkunst 7:1-2 Je 19 1932

75a ELUARD, PAUL. Donner à voir. p209-13 Paris, Gallimard, 1939
    "A Pablo Picasso," poem.

75b —— Thorns of thunder; selected poems. p20 London, Europa Press & Stanley Nott, n.d.
    "Pablo Picasso," poem translated by George Reavy.

* 76 ESTRADA, GENARO. Genio y figura de Picasso. 61 p portrait Mexico, Imprenta mundial, 1936

* 77 EVANS, MYFANWY. Beginning with Picasso. 4il Axis no2:3-5 1935

* 77a LES EXPOSITIONS DE "BEAUX-ARTS" & DE "LA GAZETTE DES BEAUX-ARTS," PARIS. Les créateurs du cubisme. 2e éd. 32p il 1935
    Exhibition catalog; preface by Maurice Raynal, chronology by Raymond Cogniat.

78 FAGUS, FÉLICIEN. Picasso. Gazette d'Art (Paris) 1901
*   Reprinted in Cahiers d'Art 7:96 1932.

79 FARGE, ADRIEN. [Preface to catalog of Picasso exhibition at B. Weill gallery, Paris] 1902
*   Reprinted in Cahiers d'Art 7:96 1932.

80 FIERENS, PAUL. Influence de Picasso sur le décor moderne. 9il Art et Décoration 61:269-78 1932

81 —— Notes sur Picasso. Le Flambeau (Brussels) 12:288-305 1929

* 82 —— Picasso and the human figure. 2il XXe siècle no5-6:39-40 1939

83 FLECHTER, RICHARD. The new Picassos. 3il Drawing and Design ns 2:170-8 1927

* 84 FLECHTHEIM, ALFRED, GALERIE, BERLIN. Pablo Picasso; zeichnungen, aquarelle, pastelle, 1902-1927. 16p 13il 1927
    Exhibition catalog. The text is a translation of 44.

85 FOLCH I TORRES, JOAQUIM. Dibuixos d'en Picasso a la col·leció Junyent. 6il Gaseta de les Arts (Barcelona) no8:1 1924

* 86 FRANKFURTER, ALFRED M. The triple celebration of Picasso. 11 il Art News 35:10-14 O 31 1936

* 87 GACETA DE ARTE (Tenerife) ns no37 1936
    Special Picasso issue, with 12 illustrations and text by Picasso, Breton, Ramón Gómez de la Serna, Eluard, Guillermo de Torre, Eduardo Westerdahl, José de la Rosa, J. Moreno Villa. Bibliography by Guillermo de Torre.

88 GASCH, SEBASTIÁ. Picasso i impressionisme. Gaseta de les Arts (Barcelona) no42:3 1926

89 GAUNT, W. Picasso and the cul-de-sac of modern painting. 7il Atelier 1 (Studio 101):408-16 Je 1931

* 90 —— Whither Picasso? 10il London Studio 17 (Studio 117):12-21 Ja 1939

* 91 GEISER, BERNHARD. Picasso, peintre-graveur; catalogue illustré de l'oeuvre gravé et lithographié, 1899-1931. 365p 257il Berne, Author, 1933

* 92 GEORGE, WALDEMAR. Aut Caesar aut nihil—reflections on the Picasso exhibition at the Georges Petit galleries. 12il Formes no25:268-71 1932

* 93 —— Les cinquante ans de Picasso, et la mort de la nature-morte. 3il Formes no 14:56 1931

* 94 —— Fair play: the passion of Picasso. 12il Formes no4:8-9 1930

95 —— Grandeur et décadence de Pablo Picasso. 12il Art Vivant 6:593-7 1930

96 —— Picasso. 12p 33il Rome, Valori Plastici, 1924
    Text in English.

* 97 —— Picasso, dessins. 15p 64il Paris, Editions des Quatre Chemins, 1926
    The text appeared in Amour de l'Art 7:189-93 1926.

98 —— Picasso et la crise actuelle de la conscience artistique. 5il Les Chroniques du Jour no2:3-10 Je 1929

99 GILLET, LOUIS. Un peintre espagnol à Paris. Revue des Deux Mondes series 8 40:562-84 1937

* 100 GOLDWATER, ROBERT J. Primitivism in modern painting. 10il p 118-25 New York, Harper, 1938

101 GOMEZ DE LA SERNA, RAMON. Completa y veridica historia de Picasso y el cubismo. 21 il Revista de Occidente 25:63-102, 224-250 Jl-Ag 1929
    English translation in Living Age 327:627-32 Ja 15 1930.

* 102 GONZALEZ, J. Picasso sculpteur; exposition de sculptures récentes de Picasso. 8il Cahiers d'Art 11 no6-7:189-91 1936

* 103 GRAHAM, J. D. Primitive art and Picasso. 8il Magazine of Art 30:236-9 Ap 1937

104 GROHMANN, WILL [Biographical sketch, with list of principal works, and bibliography] In U. Thieme and F. Becker, eds. Allgemeines lexicon der bildenden künstler 27:576-8 Leipzig, Seemann, 1932

* 105 GUÉGUEN, PIERRE. Picasso et le métapicassisme. 2il Cahiers d'Art 6:325-9 1931

106 GUILLAUME, J. P. Les papiers collés de Picasso. il Renaissance de l'Art français 21:15-16 Ja 1939

* 107 HAESAERTS, PAUL. Picasso et le goût du paroxysme. 17p 35il Anvers, Het Kompas; Amsterdam, De Spieghel, 1938

* 108 HANNOVER. KESTNER-GESELLSCHAFT. Schlemmer und Picasso. 7p il 1932
    Exhibition catalog.

* 109 HARTFORD, CONN. WADSWORTH ATHENEUM. Pablo Picasso. 15p 35il 1934
    Exhibition catalog.

* 110 HARVARD SOCIETY FOR CONTEMPORARY ART, CAMBRIDGE, MASS. Metamorphoses of P. Ovidius Naso; drawings, copper plates, etchings, artist's proofs by Pablo Ruiz Picasso. 4p 1932
    Exhibition catalog.

* 111 —— Picasso. 4p 1931
    Exhibition catalog.

112 HEILMAIER, HANS. Anmerkungen zu Pablo Picasso. 5il Deutsche Kunst und Dekoration 68:76-80 1931

113 —— Ein meister heutigen malerei: zur grossen Picasso-ausstellung in Paris. 10il Deutsche Kunst und Dekoration 70:301-8 1932
    Spanish translation in Revista de Arte (Santiago de Chile) 2no8:18-25 1936.

HENRY, DANIEL [pseud.] see KAHNWEILER, HENRY

114 HILDEBRANDT, HANS. Die frühbilder Picassos. 3il Kunst und Künstler 11:376-8 1913

BIBLIOGRAPHY

* 115 IHARA, U. Picasso 9p 37il Tokio, Atelier-Sha, 1936
Text and index in Japanese.

* 116 JACOB, MAX. Souvenirs sur Picasso. 4il Cahiers d'Art 2:199-202 1927

117 JACOBSEN, GEORG. Picasso. 7il Kunst og Kultur (Oslo) 24:1-14 1938

118 JEDLICKA, GOTTHARD. Picasso. 74p Zürich, Oprecht & Helbling, 1934
A lecture at the Zurich Kunsthaus, Oct. 1932.

119 JUNG, CARL G. Picasso [psychoanalyzed] Neue Zürcher Zeitung N 13 1932
Partial translation, with comment by Zervos, in Cahiers d'Art 7no8-10:352-4 1932.

* 120 JUSTI, LUDWIG. Von Corinth bis Klee. p 155-64 il Berlin, Bard, 1931

* 121 [KAHNWEILER, HENRY] Der weg zum kubismus, von Daniel Henry [pseud.] p 15-46 20il München,

122 KRAMÁŘ, VINCENC. Kubismus. 88p 24il Brno, Nákladem Morav.-Slezské Revue, 1921
The entire work is devoted to Picasso.

* 123 LANE, JAMES W. Picasso, the Spanish charivari. 4il Parnassus 8:16-18 N 1936

124 LANGAARD, JOHAN H. Pablo Picasso. 9il Kunst og Kultur (Oslo) 24:45-56 1938

* 125 LEICESTER GALLERIES, LONDON. Catalog of an exhibition of works by Pablo Picasso. 15p il 1921
Foreword by Clive Bell reprinted from 28.

126 LEIRIS, MICHEL. Toiles récentes de Picasso. 14il Documents 2:57-71 1930

127 LEVEL, ANDRÉ. Picasso. 58p 82il Paris, Crès, 1928

127a LEWIS, WYNDHAM. Relativism and Picasso's latest work. Blast no 1:139-40 Je 20 1914

128 LLORENS I ARTIGAS, JOSEP. Pablo Ruiz Picasso. La Revista (Barcelona) S 1923
* Reprinted in Bulletin de l'Effort Moderne no4:5-7 Ap 1924.

* 129 LONDON BULLETIN. 28il no 15-16:1-40 My 15 1939
Special issue on the exhibition "Picasso in English collections" at the London Gallery.

* 130 LOREY, EUSTACHE DE. Picasso et l'Orient musulman. 16il Gazette des Beaux-Arts series 6 2:299-314 D 1932

131 LUZZATTO, GUIDO LODOVICO. Picasso; collezione G. F. Réber. 3il Casabella 5:53-5 Je 1932

* 132 MCMAHON, MRS. AUDREY. From the sketchbook of the artist—four caricatures [by Picasso] 4il Parnassus 4:9 F 1932

* 133 MAHAUT, HENRI. Picasso. 14p 32il Paris, Crès, 1930

134 MAHRT, HAAKON BUGGE. Picasso og vor tid. 3il Konstrevy (Stockholm) p 163-6 1929

* 135 MAUNY, JACQUES. Picasso the tormentor. Magazine of Art 32:365 Je 1939

* 136 MAYOR, ALPHEUS HYATT. Picasso's method. 6il Hound & Horn 3:176-88 Winter 1930

* 137 MEIER-GRAEFE, JULIUS. Entwicklungsgeschichte der moderne kunst. 2. aufl. 3il 3:621-36 München, Piper, 1915

* 138 MELVILLE, ROBERT. Picasso, master of the phantom. 52p 12il London, Oxford University Press, 1939

† 139 MORICAND, CONRAD. Portraits astrologiques . . . Picasso. 101 p il Paris, Bellenand, 1933

140 MORTIMER, R. Picasso's work and art. 6il Architectural Review 70:21 Jl 1931

141 MURRY, JOHN MIDDLETON. The art of Pablo Picasso. The New Age (London) ns 10:115 N 30 1911

142 NASH, PAUL. Picasso and painting. Week-end Review 3:959 Je 27 1931

143 NEBESKÝ, VÁCLAV. Pablo Picasso. 8il Volné Směry (Prague) 21:110-24 1921-2

* 144 NIKODEM, V. Pablo Picasso. 12p 65il Praha, S. V. U. Mánes, 1936

* 145 OLIVIER, FERNANDE. Picasso et ses amis. 231 p 15il Paris, Stock, 1933
The text is abridged from the author's articles in Mercure de France 227:549-61; 228:558-88; 229:352-68 My 1—Jl 15 1931. Portions were translated in London Studio 7 (Studio 107):199-203 Ap 1934.

146 OPPO, CIPRIANO EFISIO. Il tramonto di Pablo Picasso. Nuova Antologia 67:324-33 O 1932

* 147 ORS, EUGENIO D'. Pablo Picasso. 62p 90il Paris, Editions des Chroniques du Jour, 1930
* Translated from the Spanish. Also an English translation, published by E. Weyhe, New York, 1930.

* 148 OZENFANT, AMÉDÉE. Foundations of modern art. p84-98 13il New York, Brewer, Warren and Putnam, 1931

* 149 —— Picasso et la peinture d'aujourd'hui. 9il L'Esprit Nouveau 2 no 13:1489-503 [1923]
Signed with the pseudonym Vauvrecy.

* 150 —— AND JEANNERET, CHARLES ÉDOUARD (LE CORBUSIER). La peinture moderne. passim 19il Paris, Crès, 1925

151 PACH, WALTER. Picasso's achievement. il Forum (New York) 73:769-75 Je 1925

* 152 PERLS GALLERIES, NEW YORK. Picasso before 1910. 4p 4il 1939
Exhibition catalog.

* 153 PERLS, KATE, GALERIE, PARIS. Picasso 1900 à 1910. 2p il 1937
Exhibition catalog.

* 154 PETIT, GEORGES, GALERIES, PARIS. Exposition Picasso. 77p 36il 1932
Exhibition catalog. Documentation by Charles Vrancken.

155 PFISTER, KURT. Ausstellung [Picasso] in der moderne galerie Thannhauser—München. 7il Deutsche Kunst und Dekoration 50:248-52 1922

* 156 PHILLIPS, VIRGINIA. Concerning Picasso's cubism. The Avenue (New York) 1:17-22, 36-40 F 5-Mr 5 1934

† 157 PICASSO, PABLO. Album de reproductions. Roma, Valori Plastici, 1913

* 158 —— Trente-deux reproductions des maquettes en couleurs d'après les originaux des costumes & décor pour le ballet Le Tricorne. 32il Paris, P. Rosenberg, 1920

* 159 PICASSO natures-mortes—still-lives—1937-39. 8il XXe siècle no5-6:55-64 1939

* 160 PIERRE, GALERIE, PARIS. Papiers collés 1912-1914 de Picasso. folder 1935
With an essay by Tristan Tzara.

161 POORE, CHARLES. The engaging old master of modernity. 10il New York Times Magazine p 10, 11, 16 N 29 1936

* 162 PROPERT, WALTER A. The Russian ballet in western Europe, 1909-20. p54-8 10il London, Lane, 1921

* 163 QUELQUES ARTISTES CONTEMPORAINS. no2 1930
Special issue on the Ballets russes. List of ballets with décor by Picasso, p32.

164 RAPHAEL, MAX. Proudhon, Marx, Picasso; trois études sur la sociologie de l'art. p 187-237 Paris, Excelsior, 1933

* 165 —— Von Monet bis Picasso. 3. aufl. p 110-18 8il München, Delphin-Verlag, 1919

* 166 RAY, MAN. Picasso photographe. 9il Cahiers d'Art 12no6-7:168-78 1937

* 167 RAYNAL, MAURICE. Anthologie de la peinture en France. p265-74 3il Paris, Editions Montaigne, 1927
*   English translation: Modern French painters. p 138-45 3il New York, Brentano's, 1928.

* 168 —— Pablo Picasso. 14p 48il Paris, Editions de l'Effort Moderne [1921]
*   Also published in a de luxe portfolio edition. The text is reprinted in Bulletin de l'Effort Moderne, no 10:8-11, no 11:5-7, no 12:6-7 D 1924—F 1925.

* 169 —— Les papiers collés de Picasso. 12il Arts et Métiers Graphiques no46:29-33 1935

170 —— Picasso. 8il Art d'Aujourd'hui p 18-24 Spring 1924

* 171 —— Picasso. 117p 101 il Paris, Crès, 1922
German translation published by Delphin-Verlag, Munich, 1921.

172 —— Picasso et l'impressionisme. 4il Amour de l'Art 2:213-16 1921

—— See also 77A

173 READ, HERBERT. Pablo Picasso. In Great contemporaries. p311-20 London, Cassell, 1935
Reprinted in the author's In defence of Shelley & other essays. p207-21. London, Heinemann, 1936.

* 174 —— Picasso's Guernica. London Bulletin no6:6 O 1938

* 175 —— The triumph of Picasso. 3il The Listener 15:1023-4 My 27 1936

* 176 REID, ALEX. & LEFEVRE, LTD., LONDON. Thirty years of Pablo Picasso. 26p 11 il 1931
Exhibition catalog.

* 177 REINHARDT GALLERIES, NEW YORK. Picasso and Derain. 2il 1930
Exhibition catalog. Foreword by James Johnson Sweeney.

178 REVERDY, PIERRE. Pablo Picasso. 16p 26il Paris, Editions de la Nouvelle Revue française, 1924

* 179 RICH, DANIEL CATTON. Consider Picasso. 3il Bulletin of the Art Institute of Chicago 25:68-71 My 1931

180 RING, GRETE. Die pariser Picasso ausstellung [bei Georges Petit] 3il Kunst und Künstler 31:286-94 1932

181 ROËLL, W. F. A. Pablo Picasso. 17il Elsevier's Geillustreerd Maandschrift (Amsterdam) 35:304-15 1925

182 ROHE, M. K. Pablo Picasso. 9il Die Kunst für Alle 28:377-83 1912-13

* 183 ROSENBERG & HELFT [ART DEALERS] LONDON. Exhibition Picasso, recent works. 4p il 1939
Exhibition catalog.

* 184 ROSENBERG, PAUL [ART DEALER] PARIS. Exposition Picasso—oeuvres récentes. 4p il 1939
Exhibition catalog.

* 185 —— Oeuvres récentes de Picasso. 12p 5il 1936
Exhibition catalog.

* 186 SABARTÉS, JAIME. Picasso, 1937. 26p il Milano, All'Insegna del Pesce d'Oro, 1937

187 SACS, JOAN. La pintura d'en Picasso. 9il Vell i Nou (Barcelona) 4:287-93, 307-10 1918

* 188 SADLER, SIR MICHAEL. Pablo Picasso. il Art Work 7:153-5 1931

BIBLIOGRAPHY

189 SALMON, ANDRÉ. L'art vivant. p 169-74 il Paris, Crès, 1920

† 190 —— La jeune peinture française. p6, 12, 14, 20, 33, 41, 51 Paris, 1912

* 191 —— La jeune sculpture française. p 103 Paris, Société des Trente, 1919

192 —— [Discussion of current criticism of Picasso in Paris] 2il Apollo 11:119-20 1930

* 193 —— Picasso. 14il L'Esprit Nouveau. 1 no 1:59-81 1920

SCHEIWILLER, GIOVANNI. See 232

194 SCHÜRER, OSKAR. Pablo Picasso. 30p 41 il Leipzig, Klinkhardt & Biermann, 1927
*   The text is a revision of the author's article in Der Cicerone 18:757-72 1926.

195 —— Picassos klassizismus. 5il Die Kunst für Alle 41:202-7 1925-26

196 SEIZE, MARC. La crise de Picasso. Les Arts Plastiques (Paris) no9 [1929?]

* 197 SELIGMANN, JACQUES & CO., NEW YORK. Picasso: "blue" and "rose" periods, 1901-1906. 24p 21 il 1936
       Exhibition catalog.

* 198 ——20 years in the evolution of Picasso, 1903-1923. 10p 17il 1937
       Exhibition catalog.

199 SITWELL, SACHEVERELL. Pablo Picasso. 7il Drawing and Design ns 1:120-5 1926

* 200 SOBY, JAMES THRALL. After Picasso. p96-9 9il Hartford, Conn., Mitchell; New York, Dodd, Mead, 1935

† 201 SOLMI, SERGIO. Pablo Picasso, der zeichner. Zürich, 1933

202 SPAINI, ALBERTO. Picasso. 6il Brescia 4:27-30 D 1931

* 203 STEIN, GERTRUDE. Autobiography of Alice B. Toklas. passim 3il New York, Harcourt, Brace, 1933

* 204 —— Dix portraits. p 15-18 Paris, Editions de la Montagne, 1930
       Text in French and English. 3 illustrations by Picasso.

* 205 —— Pablo Picasso. 7il Camera Work special no:29-30 1912

* 206 —— Picasso. 169p 63il Paris, Floury, 1938
*   English edition: Picasso. 55p 63il New York, Scribner's; London, Batsford, 1939.

207 STEIN, LEO. Pablo Picasso. New Republic 38:229-30 Ap 23 1924

* 208 SWEENEY, JAMES JOHNSON. Plastic redirections in 20th century painting. passim 9il Chicago, University of Chicago Press, 1934

—— See also 177

† 208a TÉRIADE, E. En causant avec Picasso; quelques pensées et réflexions du peintre et de l'homme. L'Intransigeant (Paris) Je 15 1932

* 209 TZARA, TRISTAN. Le papier collé; ou, Le proverbe en peinture. 12il Cahiers d'Art 6no2:61-73 1931

—— See also 160

* 210 UHDE, WILHELM. Picasso et la tradition française. passim 7il Paris, Editions des Quatre Chemins, 1928
*   English translation: Picasso and the French tradition. Paris, Editions des Quatre Chemins; New York, Weyhe, 1929.

* 211 VALENTINE GALLERY, NEW YORK. Abstractions of Picasso. 10il 1931
       Exhibition catalog.

* 212 —— Picasso. 4p 1933
       Exhibition catalog.

* 213 —— Picasso from 1901 to 1937. 2p 1937
       Exhibition catalog.

* 214 —— Picasso, 21 paintings—1908 to 1934. 2p 1938
       Exhibition catalog.

215 VANDERPYL, FRITZ R. Peintres de mon époque. p91-106 Paris, Stock, 1931

VAUVRECY [pseud.] See OZENFANT, AMÉDÉE

216 VENTURI, LIONELLO. Pablo Picasso. 10il L'Arte 36:120-40 1933

VRANCKEN, CHARLES. See 154

WARTMANN, W. See 237

* 217 WATSON, FORBES. A note on Picasso. 7il The Arts 4:332-38 1923

217a WEILL, BERTHE. Pan! dans l'oeil; ou, Trente ans dans les coulisses de la peinture contemporaine, 1900-1930. passim 2 il Paris, Lipschutz, 1933

* 218 WESTERDAHL, EDUARDO. Pablo Picasso; intellectualismo, sumisión y relacion automática de la pintura. il Gaceta de Arte (Tenerife) no 19:2-3 S 1933

* 219 WHEELER, MONROE. Meeting Picasso. il University Review 3:175-9 Spring 1937

220 WILENSKI, R. H. [Review of E. d'Ors, Picasso] Apollo 13:187-90 1931

* 221 ZAHAR, MARCEL. Picasso; la danse dans la peinture contemporaine. Archives Internationales de Danse p94-9 D 1933

* 222 ZAHN, LEOPOLD. Picasso und der kubismus. 13il Jahrbuch der Jungen Kunst 3:116-30 1922

* 223 —— Picasso und Kandinsky. Ararat (Munich) 2:171-3 1920

ZAYAS, MARIUS DE. See DE ZAYAS, MARIUS

* 224 ZERVOS, CHRISTIAN. De l'importance de l'objet dans la peinture d'aujourd'hui. 48il Cahiers d'Art 5no5:225-40, 5no6:281-94 1930

* 225 —— La dernière exposition de Picasso [à la galerie Paul Rosenberg] 12il Cahiers d'Art 14 no 1-4:81-8 1939

* 226 —— Dernières oeuvres de Picasso. 12il Cahiers d'Art 2:189-98 1927

* 227 —— Dernières oeuvres de Picasso. 26il Cahiers d'Art 4:233-50 1929

* 228 —— Histoire de l'art contemporain. p 193-222 27il Paris, Editions des Cahiers d'Art, 1938

* 229 —— Lendemain d'une exposition. 4il Cahiers d'Art 1:119-21 1926

* 230 —— Oeuvres récentes de Picasso. 8il Cahiers d'Art 1:89-93 1926

* 231 —— Pablo Picasso; works from 1895 to 1906. 35p 384il New York, Weyhe; Paris, Editions des Cahiers d'Art, 1932

* 232 —— Pablo Picasso. 26p 30il Milano, Hoepli, 1932
Text in Italian. Bibliography by Giovanni Scheiwiller.

* 233 —— Picasso à Dinard, été 1928. 27il Cahiers d'Art 4:5-20 1929

* 234 ——Picasso; oeuvres 1920-1926. 19p 47il Paris, Editions des Cahiers d'Art, 1926

* 235 ——Picasso; oeuvres inédites anciennes. 29il Cahiers d'Art 3:204-27 1928

* 236 —— Projets de Picasso pour un monument. 13il Cahiers d'Art 4:342-54 1929

—— See also 38-40

* 237 ZURICH. KUNSTHAUS. Picasso. 25p 32il 1932
Exhibition catalog. Foreword by W. Wartmann.

* 238 ZWEMMER GALLERY, LONDON. Fifty drawings by Pablo Picasso. folder [1937]
Exhibition catalog.

TEN THOUSAND COPIES OF THIS BOOK HAVE BEEN PRINTED
FOR THE TRUSTEES OF THE MUSEUM OF MODERN ART IN
NOVEMBER 1939 BY WILLIAM E. RUDGE'S SONS, NEW YORK